CRIME, COMMUNITY AND LOCALE

Crime, Community and Locale
The Northern Ireland Communities Crime Survey

DAVID O'MAHONY
RAY GEARY
KIERAN McEVOY
JOHN MORISON
Institute of Criminology and Criminal Justice,
School of Law, The Queen's University of Belfast

LONDON AND NEW YORK

First published 2000 by Ashgate Publishing

Reissued 2018 by Routledge
2 Park Square, Milton Park, Abingdon, Oxon OX14 4RN
711 Third Avenue, New York, NY 10017, USA

Routledge is an imprint of the Taylor & Francis Group, an informa business

Copyright © David O'Mahony, Ray Geary, Kieran McEvoy and John Morison 2000

All rights reserved. No part of this book may be reprinted or reproduced or utilised in any form or by any electronic, mechanical, or other means, now known or hereafter invented, including photocopying and recording, or in any information storage or retrieval system, without permission in writing from the publishers.

Notice:
Product or corporate names may be trademarks or registered trademarks, and are used only for identification and explanation without intent to infringe.

Publisher's Note
The publisher has gone to great lengths to ensure the quality of this reprint but points out that some imperfections in the original copies may be apparent.

Disclaimer
The publisher has made every effort to trace copyright holders and welcomes correspondence from those they have been unable to contact.

A Library of Congress record exists under LC control number: 00132847

ISBN 13: 978-1-138-72971-1 (hbk)
ISBN 13: 978-1-138-72965-0 (pbk)
ISBN 13: 978-1-315-18974-1 (ebk)

Table of Contents

List of Tables   viii
Preface   xi

1   **Introduction**   1
     Background to Local Community Crime Surveys   4
     The Notion of Community   5
     Governmentality and the Crime Survey   7
     Outline of Book Structure   9

2   **Perceptions of the Communities**   12
     The Communities   12
     Problems in the Communities   16
     The Top Five Issues in the Communities   25
     Satisfaction with the Communities   27
     Conclusions   30

3   **Crime and Victimisation in the Communities**   34
     Introduction   34
     Crime and Victimisation   35
     Reporting Crime to the Police   43
     Reasons For Not Reporting Incidents to the Police   47
     Witnessing Crime   49
     Conclusions   52

4   **Worries and Fears in the Communities**   56
     Introduction   56
     General Fear of Crime   57
     Worry about Specific Incidents   61
     Perceptions of Crime in Northern Ireland and Elsewhere   66
     Conclusions   70

5	**Policing and the Communities**	74
	Introduction	74
	General Levels of Satisfaction with the Police	75
	Reporting Crime to the Police	77
	Personal Knowledge of Police Officers	79
	Fairness of the Police	80
	The Importance of Police Tasks	81
	Crime Management and 'Other' Organisations	83
	Conclusions	87
6	**Securing the Home**	90
	Introduction	90
	Crime Prevention	92
	Empty Properties	96
	Insurance	97
	Means of Reducing Crime	98
	Conclusions	101
7	**Children in Public Space**	104
	Introduction	104
	General Evaluations of Children's Safety	106
	Particular Parental Concerns	112
	Children's Activities: Family and Civil Society	115
	Conclusions	118
8	**Governmentality, Communities and Crime**	120
	Crime, Safety and Governmentality	121
	Communities, Patten and Crime	127
	Security and Control	129

Appendix 1

	Survey Design and Methodology	132
	Selection of the Communities	132
	Criteria Used to Select the Communities	134
	Interviews and Response Rates	136
	Representativeness of the Sample	140

Appendix 2
    The Questionnaire   143

Bibliography   186

List of Tables

Table 2.1	Choice of Community Types Included in the Survey	14
Table 2.2	Respondents' Views Regarding Broad Social Problems in their Areas	18
Table 2.3	Respondents' Views Regarding Environmental Problems/ Living Space Issues in their Area	20
Table 2.4	Respondents' Views Regarding Environmental Problems/Issues of Disorder in their Area	22
Table 2.5	Respondents' Views Regarding Crime in their Area	23
Table 2.6	Respondents' Views Regarding Harassment in their Area	25
Table 2.7	Top Five Issues that People Considered to be a 'Big Problem' or a 'Bit of a Problem' in the Areas at Present	27
Table 2.8	Respondents' Views Regarding the Type of Community in which they Live	29
Table 3.1	Per Cent of Respondents Victimised by Any Type of Crime in the Previous Twelve Months	37
Table 3.2	Per Cent of Respondents Victimised by Household Crime in the Previous Twelve Months	38
Table 3.3	Per Cent of Respondents Victimised by Personal Crime in the Previous Twelve Months	39
Table 3.4	Per Cent of Respondents Victimised by Vehicle Crime in the Previous Twelve Months	40

Table 3.5	Respondents Victimised by Sectarian Crime in the Previous Twelve Months	42
Table 3.6	Per Cent of Respondents Reporting Household Victimisation to the Police	43
Table 3.7	Per Cent of Respondents Reporting Personal Crime	44
Table 3.8	Per Cent of Respondents Reporting Vehicle Crime	45
Table 3.9	Per Cent of Respondents Reporting Sectarian Crime	46
Table 3.10	Main Reason for Not Reporting Incident to the Police	48
Table 3.11	Per Cent of Respondents Witnessing Crime in their Areas over the Past Three Years	50
Table 3.12	Per Cent of Respondents who had Witnessed Crime and Reported it to the Police	52
Table 4.1	Respondents' Fear of Crime - Day and Night-time	60
Table 4.2	Respondents' Worries about Burglary, Assaults and Threats	61
Table 4.3	Respondents' Worries about Theft and Vandalism of a Vehicle	63
Table 4.4	Respondents' Worries about Sectarian Crime - Home Damage, Physical Attack and Terrorist Attack	65
Table 4.5	Respondents' Perceptions of the Relative Extent of Ordinary Crime in the Communities in Comparison to the Rest of Northern Ireland, Great Britain and the Republic of Ireland	68
Table 4.6	Respondents' Perceptions of the Extent of Crime in the Communities and in Northern Ireland generally During the Period of the Cease-fires	69
Table 5.1	Respondents' Levels of Satisfaction with the RUC, Housing Executive and Street Cleaning Department	76
Table 5.2	Percentage of Respondents stating that they would 'Very Likely' Report the Incident to the Police	78

Table 5.3	Respondents' Personal Knowledge of the Police	80
Table 5.4	Respondents' Views Regarding Police Fairness in the Treatment of People in Northern Ireland as a Whole	81
Table 5.5	Respondents' Views Regarding the Importance of Police Tasks	82
Table 5.6	Respondents' Reporting to Other Organisations Dealing with Crime in Their Area	84
Table 5.7	Respondents Reporting that Other Organisations were Involved in Dealing with Certain Crime Related Issues	86
Table 6.1	Security Measures in the Home	92
Table 6.2	Installing Home Security	94
Table 6.3	Property Left Empty	96
Table 6.4	Home Insurance	98
Table 6.5	Reducing Crime	100
Table 7.1	Good Area to Bring Up Children	107
Table 7.2	Children's Safety	108
Table 7.3	Allowing Children Out Alone – Day/Night	109
Table 7.4	Extent of Worry when Children are Outside	110
Table 7.5	Particular Worries	113
Table 7.6	Particular Worries	114
Table 7.7	Worry During Cease-fires	115
Table 7.8	Activities out of School Hours	117
Table A.1	Choice of Community Types Included in the Survey	133
Table A.2	Number of Wards and Interviews Selected for each of the Community Types	136
Table A.3	Completion Rates by Community Types	139
Table A.4	Average Deprivation Rank Order Scores for Community Types	141
Table A.5	Religious Division by Community Types (per cent): 1991 Census Data and Survey Respondents	141
Table A.6	Sex by Community Type (per cent): 1991 Census Data and Survey Respondents	142
Table A.7	Age by Community Type (per cent): 1991 Census Data and Survey Respondents	142

Preface

This book is about ordinary life in Northern Ireland. It goes behind the headlines of violence and political conflict to examine how people in a range of communities within Northern Ireland experience a whole series of factors relating to crime, policing and, indeed, the general experience of living within their particular communities. There have always been ordinary lives lived out behind the headlines but now the Peace Process, whatever vicissitudes it may undergo, has changed life massively and irrevocably. Some more obvious problems have receded but there are new challenges in adjusting to the new society that is promised. The survey that is at the heart of this account, offers a snapshot of this process of change and adjustment as it was being experienced across a variety of communities in what remains a 'divided society'.

The process of change is far from over and there is a long way to go before Northern Ireland can relax with only the problems and challenges of so-called 'ordinary' crime and policing. However, the journey is underway and this book indicates how some of the central issues that must be resolved are perceived by a range of ordinary people in various urban and rural communities, in religiously segregated and integrated communities and by those with different levels of income and social infrastructure. The sound of authentic voices can be heard here and these deserve to be heard. The experiences and attitudes gathered are important in understanding how the process of change and development in this society might be advanced and what lessons might be offered to elsewhere.

Beyond the immediate context of Northern Ireland, the Communities Crime Survey that is reported here has a resonance for anyone interested in how to connect the experiences of everyday living with some of the concerns of criminology and the criminal justice system. There are new innovations here in terms of survey methodology and some important arguments are engaged with. But beyond the concerns of academic criminology there is here a democratic exercise whereby ordinary people have been given their say. We believe that what they have said is worth listening to.

Many people were instrumental in the process of funding, designing and executing the survey and in producing this work. We are grateful to all of them and, in particular, The Northern Ireland Office who funded the original study, Tom Haire, Dr Debbie Donnelly, Professor Mike Brogden, Dr Brian MacLean, Peter Ward of Research and Evaluation Services and his survey team, Katie Quinn, Brian Hollywood, Professor Stephen Livingstone and all the many others who so kindly gave their help.

DO'M, RG, KMcE and JM
Belfast, February 2000

1 Introduction

This book reports the findings of the first communities based crime survey carried out within Northern Ireland. The survey asked a number of questions beyond the usual remit of local crime surveys in order to explore more fully a whole range of issues relating to the experience of living in a society where the more obvious manifestations of conflict are beginning to recede and other more mundane but still important issues relating to crime and policing are coming to the fore. The production of this book coincides with dramatic changes to the political, social and criminological framework of Northern Ireland. Following the conclusion of the multi-party talks in April 1998, and the enactment of the Northern Ireland Act 1998 detailing structures for devolved government, there has been a movement towards restoring 'normal' political conditions in the jurisdiction. Along with the large-scale political changes there has been a concomitant process of review in the areas of criminal justice and policing. Mechanisms have been put in place to secure the early release of the vast majority of paramilitary prisoners and provisions for victims of the conflict have been considered. These changes reflect the fact that life in Northern Ireland is poised to change in fundamental ways and will hopefully emerge as, in the words of the Independent Commission on Policing, 'a community at peace with itself and committed to the democratic process' (Patten, 1999 p. 1).

The centrality of issues of crime, security and policing to the process of conflict resolution reflects the fact that such matters lay at the very heart of the three decades of political violence. The fact that many of these issues are now being addressed anew, paradoxically presents opportunities for fresh and innovative approaches to basic issues that elsewhere are frozen in politicised or technocratic debates on crime management (Currie, 1998; Beckett and Sasson, 1999; Crawford, 1999; Garland, 1996). There is now a real opportunity to address and resolve issues beyond the macro political level and develop ideas about how basic issues of crime and policing ought to be addressed at a community level in the new Northern Ireland.

One key part of the contested nature of the conflict has related to images and discourses concerning ordinary crime as well as political violence. As elsewhere, crime rates in particular have been deployed in an explicitly political fashion (Brownlee, 1998; Ryan, 1999). However, the intensity of the conflict in Northern Ireland meant that the significance of this politicisation process over crime rates considerably augmented their importance.

Drawing upon such information as was available, two competing theses about the level of crime in Northern Ireland emerged (see further, Morison and Geary, 1989). The first, originating with those interested in the psychological casualties of the 'Troubles', gained currency during the 1970s. This suggested a process whereby violence from the political context became generalised to other areas of life in a pattern of escalating crime where new generations infected by the disruption of the political conflict replaced the older more law-abiding population. There is some evidence of this view gaining official currency with a moral panic developing among policy makers over juvenile crime (Caul, 1983) and government taking precautions to avoid a crisis of anti-social behaviour (Powell, 1982).

Of course this 'breakdown of the social fabric' thesis depended upon denying the validity of the official statistics which generally showed lower rates of crime in Northern Ireland than in the rest of the UK. This was done by questioning whether hostility to the police within some sections of the community, and sympathy towards them in others, combined with paramilitary activity in policing certain areas to produce lower reporting rates. This early view was framed within a wider perspective which located blame with the paramilitary forces who had ruptured the social and political fabric of a traditional society. Reference to crime rates and social disorder provided the material that was used to fashion this thesis.

The other thesis, emerging during the 1980s and gaining currency since then, suggests that there may in fact be a 'surprisingly low rate' in Northern Ireland despite the 'Troubles'. Although there are high levels of relative deprivation which might suggest high levels of crime[1], this thesis maintains that the fabric of society in Northern Ireland has not broken

---

[1] Even now in a relatively improving economy which has lost its Objective One status as an area of particular need with the European Union, more than one fifth of household income comes from social security benefits which is a higher proportion than anywhere else in the UK (Office for National Statistics 1997).

down and that levels of what the security forces term 'ordinary decent crime' remain low compared with elsewhere in the United Kingdom (Heskin, 1981). This view was supported by what statistical evidence was then available from the Chief Constable's Annual Reports and the Northern Ireland Office's *Commentaries on Northern Ireland Crime Statistics*. These measures were used to support the assertion that underneath a veneer provided by 'the men of violence', Northern Ireland was a decent, church-going, family oriented society with low rates of ordinary decent crime - a 'paradise on earth' as one former Tory minister described it (Patten, 1996). The measurement of crime rates became a political tool to pathologise and obscure the political origins of paramilitary crime. Only a very uncritical view of there being 'two communities' engaged an age-old, sectarian squabble with little appreciation of the role of the state as anything other than a neutral and ultimately benign umpire.

Since the emergence of these two conflicting theses, the level of available information has changed dramatically. In 1989 Northern Ireland was included in the International Crime Survey, (Van Dijk *et al.*, 1990) although not the 1992 version (van Dijk and Mayhew, 1992). Northern Ireland was also included in the 1996 International Crime Victims Survey (ICVS) (Mayhew and van Dijk, 1997) and a Northern Ireland wide crime survey was conducted in-house by the NIO in 1994/5, selected extracts of which have now been published (Boyle and Haire, 1996). In addition, there are a large number of on-going public opinion surveys carried out on behalf of organisations such as the Police Authority for Northern Ireland (e.g. PANI, 1998).

However, some of the major questions raised by the original two competing theses about crime in Northern Ireland have not been answered. Both these, and the political premises that they predicated, were based upon a holistic view of Northern Ireland inhabited by 'averaged up' citizens who remained largely undifferentiated beyond the two major religious blocks (Catholics/Protestants)[2]. Little room was afforded to important and defining variables and other important localised factors.

---

[2] For example, in an otherwise unremarkable article about the role of the voluntary sector in Northern Ireland, one commentator from outside the jurisdiction stated in a way that is illustrative of this tendency: 'In Northern Ireland, there are, of course, many ways to determine communities than along the lines of Protestantism and Catholicism. However, for the purposes of the Article, community development will be considered within the context of these two alone'. Shense J (1999).

In contrast, the survey described in this book takes the view that Northern Ireland is neither a homogeneous entity nor a society that is simply divided on religious and/or political grounds. Rather it is a society that is divided by religion and politics, but also by a number of other variables - including geography (particularly the urban/rural divide), gender, age, socio-economic class and ethnic origin - all of which will in part influence people's experiences and attitudes to crime and policing[3]. While this study does appear to confirm the relatively low levels of victimisation suggested in previous research, it was also found that there were significant variations to be found in the different communities as regards experiences and attitudes to crime and policing. This research also seeks to relate crime to a broader spectrum of nuisance and anti-social activity i.e. 'quality of life' issues as opposed to simply law-breaking. Similarly, in terms of the response to crime, the research seeks to explore not only whether or not people call the police but whether they engage in a range of 'problem-solving' techniques either involving their own actions or those of their family, their community or other aspects of civil society.

Background to Local Community Crime Surveys

The developments within criminology over the past twenty years, which have seen ever greater specificity in the data available for analysis, have been well covered elsewhere (Bottomley and Pease, 1986; Maguire, 1997) and it is unnecessary to reproduce them in detail here. Suffice to say that in the USA and Britain national victimisation surveys were conceived from the late 1960s through to the early 1980s as a method for estimating the frequency and distribution of unreported crime (Ennis, 1967; Hood and Sparks, 1970; Hough and Mayhew, 1983; Chambers and Tombs, 1984). These surveys confirmed that considerable numbers of crimes went unreported (the 'dark figure of crime'). They stressed that, in fact, most crime was petty and that the risks of being victimised were statistically improbable (Hough and Mayhew, 1983). For example, the 1983 British Crime Survey argued that a 'statistically average person' aged 16 or over can expect a robbery every five centuries, an assault once every century, a

---

[3] Not all of these variables are reported in this book. Consideration is limited to the dimensions of socio-economic deprivation, religious division and urbanisation in different communities.

car to be stolen once every 60 years and a burglary once every fifty years (Hough and Mayhew, 1983, p. 168).

Some commentators suggested that such surveys were guilty of distorting the 'real' experiences of crime of particular groupings such as the poor, ethnic minorities and women (Matthews and Young, 1986; Stanko, 1988) and of denigrating fear of crime amongst such vulnerable groupings as 'irrational' (Young, 1988). Such 'left realist' commentators argued that there were considerable differences in the experience of crime and policing between and within different areas, triggered by such issues as gender, ethnicity and socio-economic status (MacLean, 1991; Young, 1997). Commissioned by Labour councils with a particular interest in police accountability (Currie, DeKerskey and MacLean, 1990), local surveys were carried out in a range of British cities including Islington (Jones *et al.*, 1986; Crawford *et al.*, 1990), Merseyside (Kinsey, 1984) and Dundee (Jones *et al.*, 1994)[4]. While left realist local survey work has been criticised on a number of grounds (DeKerskey, MacLean and Schwart, 1997), it is the complexity of the notion of 'community' upon which they predicate much that is perhaps most relevant to discussions of the Northern Ireland Community Crime Survey.

The Notion of Community

Crawford (1995; 1999) has described the notion of community as 'both a signifier and a referent around which complex and contradictory effects, meanings and definitional struggles coalesce'. It is a concept, which, while it lacks definitional precision (Butcher, 1993, p. 3; Crawford, 1999), is nonetheless of huge significance to a broad range of disciplines including geography, political science, sociology, social policy, psychology, women's studies and others - 'all of which have recognised a tendency to use the word uncritically as a blanket which 'means all things to all people' (Dalley, 1988, p. 48). Community has been described as 'interlocking social networks of neighbourhood, kinship and friendship' (Crow and

---

[4] The British Crime Survey has, perhaps in response to the perceived failure to reach certain groupings, also augmented its scope by including additional 'booster' samples in order to elicit a wider perspective of experiences. In 1988, for example, it contained for the first time an additional 'booster' example of Afro-Caribbean's and Asians.

Allan, 1994, p. 178-179), and as something shared in common between people whether in terms of territoriality, ethnicity, religious background or occupational or leisure pursuits (Willmott, 1986). Communities may in effect be socially constructed (Cohen, 1985), playing an important symbolic role in encouraging and maintaining a sense of belonging in particular by identifying boundaries that define who is and who is not a member of the community (Cohen, 1987, p. 14).

Within criminological discourse, community has often been considered more narrowly than in other disciplines. It has been described as having at least three meanings within criminological work (Walklate, 1996), all of which were of relevance to our Northern Ireland Communities Crime Survey (NICCS).

Firstly, there is the idea of *disorganised community*. Inspired by the Chicago school emphasis on zones of transition in a changing urban setting, such a view suggests that a lack of community infrastructure, developed social and familial networks and shared norms contribute to criminal behaviour (Shaw and McKay, 1942). The corresponding conclusion of such analysis is, of course, that the presence of a developed community infrastructure and networks of social control suggest a well-balanced, low crime rate society.

Such ideas are closely related to a second sense of *community as social cement*. This develops the negative sense of community disappearing, and turns it into a more positive, communitarian or authoritarian thesis that 'community values' should be restored - by government action if necessary. Within such a viewpoint, Northern Ireland can serve as an indicator of how traditional values can be deployed to resist the spread of crime. This may at first sight appear strange, and it is certainly contrary to the image that is portrayed within popular culture (Geary and Morison, 1996). However, this supports the thesis that Northern Ireland society, despite or perhaps because of its 'Troubles', has missed out on many of the influences which elsewhere have eroded family and church ties. An exploration of community in this sense is important in so far as it may assist in interrogating the assumptions behind how the 'decline into lawlessness' thesis of 1970s has been replaced in 1980s and 1990s by a 'surprisingly low crime rate' thesis (Morison, 1995).

Thirdly, there is the idea of a *disadvantaged community*. Such an idea can be found in the work of Hope and Shaw (1988) developing the ideas of Cloward and Ohlin (1960) amongst others. This advances the idea that crime, particularly juvenile crime, arises because of disparity between material aspirations which popular culture suggests to young people and their concrete circumstances. The ability to achieve such goals is blocked by practical structural impediments such as social class, ethnicity or lack of employment opportunities. In the Northern Ireland context, where relative levels of deprivation are very varied, the implications of exploring how communities vary depending on degrees of deprivation and relative affluence are of considerable interest.

Conscious of the problematic notion of community, the Community Crime Survey sought to go beyond much of the official and media discourse, centred as it is on discussion of the two principle religious blocks (the Protestant and Catholic 'communities') as more or less homogenous entities. Such a focus was not designed to obfuscate the differential views or experiences of Catholics or Protestants on crime and policing. Rather, religious division was viewed as one variable which is intersected by a number of others including socio-economic status, geographical setting and sense of community. People live, socialise and bring up their children in different communities, and view themselves as belonging to different communities based on the whole range of variables discussed above. Individuals' experiences and attitudes are determined therefore not simply by what they themselves directly encounter, but by the experiences, attitudes, values and self-image of 'their' community, however defined.

Governmentality and the Crime Survey

In a recent article, Garland has highlighted how 'the governmentality literature offers a powerful framework for analysing how crime is problematized and controlled' (1997, p.174). This literature has developed over the past twenty years in response to Foucault's later writings, lectures and interviews on the topic. By the time of his death in 1984, however, Foucault had not fully developed his project on governmentality. We are therefore left with some specific writings on the theme, notably 'Governmentality' (1991) and 'The Subject and Power' (1982), and a rich seam of lines of inquiry that remain suggestive rather than fully realised. The themes that Foucault introduced, however, have been taken up by a number of writers who have considered various aspects of governmental concerns. Though they differ in some aspects of their analysis (see, for example, Burchell *et al.*, 1991; Rose and Miller, 1992; Barry *et al.*, 1993; O'Malley *et al.*, 1997; Smandych, 1999), they employ the same conceptual tools in anatomizing the actions of government. It is these tools that we have sought to utilize in analysing how crime is perceived and how it effects individuals in different communities in Northern Ireland; how these individuals perceive and respond to governmental actions on crime and policing; and how governmental actions may be effected by those responses in the different communities, particularly in the manner in which they are considered in 'The Report of the Independent Commission on Policing for Northern Ireland' (Patten, 1999).

The approach that the writers on governmentality share is a rejection of the notion of government as being synonymous with the state, and of power emanating simply from a sovereign monolith. Instead, power is exercised at a distance, diffused through a diverse number of sites, both traditional, in the sense of the police and the criminal justice system, and extended, by way of families, experts, professions, counsellors, churches and so on, who are all concerned with the 'conduct of conduct'. This was one of the twin facets of government that Foucault was concerned with, the means by which individuals govern, conduct themselves, and so shape their own subjectivity. The other facet was in terms of the government of others in the political domain, and equally important, the interconnections that exist between the two forms of government. For, 'the exercise of power consists in guiding the possibility of conduct and putting in order the possible outcome' (Foucault, 1982, p. 222).

The governmentality literature eschews a historical or sociological approach, not being concerned with attempting to construct what may have actually happened in the past or revealing the actuality of present day government through a substantive account of its workings and motivations. Instead it is concerned with looking at the practices of governance in different areas at a micro level and how they come about through specific ways of thinking, 'rationalities', and specific ways of acting, 'technologies'. These rationalities and technologies are then subjected to a 'genealogical' analysis - 'a tracing of their historical lineages that aims to undermine their "naturalness" and open up a space for alternative possibilities' (Garland, 1997, p.174). In this way the rationalities of rule that have been applied at different times, classical liberalism, welfarism, neo-liberalism, can be examined and the means by which specific government programmes are translated into practical government analysed. The approach is concerned with how government is thought into being in programmatic form, how the practitioners of rule ask themselves the question of how best to govern, what concepts they invent or deploy to render their subjects governable in certain ways, and how government constantly reforms itself in light of failures and evaluations' (O'Malley *et al.*, 1997, p. 502). In the governmenality literature, however, the notion of 'failure', in the sense of the unsuccessful implementation of a programme due to the intransigence of the subject to whom the programme is applied is a contested point. For some, for example Miller and Rose (1990), it has only a negative value, insofar as it involves an obstacle to the successful implementation of a government programme that then requires the programmers to rectify the perceived fault, albeit that the resulting programme may be more efficient from the programmers perspective. The alternative perspective is provided by O'Malley *et al.*, who argue that there is 'abundant evidence that contestations, resistances and social antagonisms shape rule through systematic provision of alternatives' (1997, p. 510). Such a perspective provides a far richer potential for the governmentality literature (see, for example, O'Malley, 1996*b*; Weir, 1996) especially when it is applied to the issue of policing in Northern Ireland and the government initiatives of the past compared to the rationality adopted in the Patten Report. This governmentality perspective, and its importance within the Patten Report provides a framework through which the Community Crime Survey can be viewed. It will be returned to explicitly in the final chapter.

Outline of Book Structure

In chapter two the differing communities chosen for inclusion in this survey are examined in relation to how individuals from these areas see their environment and a whole range of physical, social and environmental conditions within them. It is shown that conditions and experiences across the communities differ greatly. For example, in terms of the physical make-up of the communities, those living in the urban lower working class areas reported considerably higher levels of dissatisfaction with their environment, from poor housing to inadequate amenities in their areas. It is also apparent that many of the problems that exist in the communities are linked into the local conditions within them. Many of those in the lower working class areas saw unemployment as a major problem for their area, while very few of those from the middle class areas regarded it as a problem. The issues also extend into problems of public order and disputes whereby those in the lower working class areas reported many more difficulties like disturbances from teenagers, public drunkenness or neighbourhood disputes. One of the most important points that emerges from this chapter is the importance of community in relation to physical and social conditions and how much these differ at a local level. It is argued that the importance of understanding local conditions and the environment in which people live is central to gaining an insight of their attitudes and experiences.

The third chapter explores the extent to which crime and victimisation occurred across the differing communities. While levels of victimisation found were relatively low it was evident that patterns and rates of victimisation differed across the communities. This was especially so between those living in the small town communities and those living in the urban areas. It was also clear that there were differences in the types of crimes experienced across the communities. Indeed, differences were noted in the rates of reporting crimes to the police and the reasons given for not reporting incidents. Those from the Catholic lower working class communities were found to be the most reluctant to report incidents to the police and they gave differing reasons for failing to report incidents. The chapter shows not only differing patterns of victimisation across the communities, but the extent to which crime problems may be very localised.

The fourth chapter looks at the issue of worries and fear of crime. Here, it is shown how communities and the environment in which people live have an important impact on worries and levels of fear of crime. It is suggested that to properly understand the issue of fear of crime it is necessary to locate the individual in their environment. This means not only looking at the individual's characteristics, such as their age, sex and class, but looking at where they live and the environmental conditions they find themselves in when trying to explain and understand such worries.

Chapter five goes on to examine the experiences and attitudes of those in the various communities with regard to policing. As is discussed, much of the previous survey data on community attitudes towards policing in Northern Ireland has focused upon the relatively high levels of satisfaction with the RUC (e.g. PANI, 1996) with Catholic/Nationalists generally less supportive and less positive than their Protestant/Unionist counterparts. The emphasis in much of this data has been almost exclusively on the divergences between Catholics and Protestants (McGarry and O'Leary, 1999). This chapter suggests that while religion/political opinion is a key variable in understanding views and experiences of policing, insufficient account has been taken of other variables such as class or geographical area. The chapter explores levels of satisfaction amongst the communities with regard to the police, police performance, whether respondents felt people were treated fairly and whether respondents would make use of the police in response to a range of hypothetical events. Finally the chapter concludes with an analysis of the role of alternative community based sources of help in dealing with crime and anti-social behaviour including paramilitary groupings in the various communities.

The sixth chapter argues that with the improved security situation, a changing role for the RUC, and a rise in ordinary crime, there is a new emphasis on crime prevention measures. This is both in terms of granting it a higher priority within the RUC and an increased emphasis on the responsibility of individual householders to increase their own security. These developments are examined in the context of different community attitudes on adopting crime prevention measures, the role of insurance and the best means of reducing crime in the communities.

Chapter seven examines children's safety in public space within the various communities. Parents were asked about their concerns for their children in various age groups in order to explore feelings about the dangers and risks attaching to a range of activities that children are involved in during their leisure time. The nature and extent of particular worries are considered. Wider issues about the importance of particular spaces, both within a home environment and within public and communal areas, and the sense of security that parents have in relation to their children in such spaces, are examined. The use of civic amenities, as well as more privatised facilities within public space, is explored. Attention is also given to the degree to which and the way in which children's activity is organised both by elements of civil society including friends and church groupings.

The final chapter returns to the issue of governmentality and seeks to relate the issues of the Community Crime Survey to the new possibilities in Northern Ireland as indicated in the Independent Commission on Policing (Patten 1999).

2 Perceptions of the Communities

The Communities

As this research is very much centred around exploring the extent to which differing community conditions impact upon the lives and experiences of those living in such circumstances, the researchers set out to pick areas that were very distinct from each other. This was informed to a large extent by the previous literature which shows the importance of understanding local circumstances and conditions when trying to explain the distribution of crime and victimisation (e.g. Sparks *et al.*, 1977; Bottoms, 1987; Jones *et al.*, 1986; Anderson *et al.*, 1990; Crawford, 1999). Much of this research demonstrates how many social problems and difficulties are related to specific environmental conditions and localities. For example, community based crime surveys like those conducted in Islington (Jones *et al.*, 1986; Crawford *et al.*, 1990) and Merseyside (Kinsey, 1985) found considerably higher levels of some forms of victimisation than national surveys suggest, especially when compared to the British Crime Survey (BCS) results. Significantly, these surveys show how urban areas with high levels of social and economic deprivation are especially prone to crime. They also show how those living in certain areas or communities are often more likely to be exposed to a whole range of adverse experiences beyond crime; poor housing, overcrowded living conditions, problems with litter and graffiti, to poor social and environmental facilities - all of which may well negatively affect their quality of life. Indeed the Dundee Victim Survey (Jones *et al.*, 1994) which concentrated on a number of run-down council estates, shows the extent to which crime and social problems are correlated with areas of intense socio-economic deprivation.

The impact of community based variables beyond the urban environment has also been examined and studies have been conducted exploring the effects of the urban/rural divide. The Aberystwyth Crime Survey (Koffman, 1993), for example, found that crime and victimisation was considerably lower in rural communities than national figures suggest. Moreover, results from a recent sweep of the British Crime Survey (BCS), when analysed across urban and rural areas, show not only lower risks of victimisation, but less social and physical disorder in rural than urban areas (Mirrlees-Black, 1998).

Our Northern Ireland Communities Crime Survey then, in contrast to much of the national victimisation survey work, seeks to explore the extent to which differing community types in Northern Ireland impact upon those who live within such areas, and how such experiences may actually be tied into differing social and environmental conditions. To achieve this a number of community types were identified from previous research as being of particular interest. Such communities include socio-economically disadvantaged, run-down areas versus affluent, thriving and well-kept communities; communities in large urban areas versus those in rural or small-town areas; and, as a result of the particular problems in Northern Ireland, where there is a high degree of religious segregation and conflict, communities that are extremely religiously segregated versus those that are more religiously integrated.

From these considerations, three broad community groupings were established which can be seen in Table 2.1 below. The community groupings are: a) the large, urban, lower working-class, religiously segregated communities; b) large, urban, upper middle-class, religiously mixed communities; and c) small-town, lower middle-class and religiously divided communities. From these three groupings, five actual community types emerged which are used throughout the rest of this research. They include: 1) the large, urban, predominantly Catholic, lower working-class communities; 2) large, urban, predominantly Protestant lower working-class communities; 3) large, urban, mixed religion, upper middle-class communities; 4) small-town, predominately Catholic, lower middle-class communities, and; 5) the small-town, predominantly Protestant lower middle-class communities (see Table 2.1 below).

For the five community types noted above, a number of electoral wards were chosen to represent each of the communities. The wards were carefully selected using objective criteria. Face to face interviews, employing computer-assisted interviewing techniques, were conducted with randomly selected respondents in each of the selected wards (see Appendix 1 for further details). The selection of the wards was made using data from a range of independent sources such as the Northern Ireland

Census (1991) to determine the religious composition of the wards, Northern Ireland Ordnance Survey maps to choose wards according to their size, housing density and geographical location, and a recent comprehensive index of relative deprivation carried out across all the wards of Northern Ireland (Robson, 1994). Thus the selection procedures allowed for an objective and scientific process to be utilised in the choice of wards representing the community types under examination.

Table 2.1   Choice of Community Types Included in the Survey

A		B	C	
Urban, Lower Working Class Religiously Divided		Urban Middle Class Mixed Religiously	Small Town Middle Class Religiously Divided	
1	2	3	4	5
Catholic Lower Working Class Urban	Protestant Lower Working Class Urban	Mixed Religion Upper Middle Class Urban	Catholic Small Town	Protestant Small Town
4 Wards n=312	3 Wards n=290	3 Wards n=441	2 Wards n=286	2 Wards n=292

For the urban lower working-class, religiously divided communities, seven wards were selected in the Belfast area. They were chosen to give a good geographical spread across the city, so as to avoid focusing in on just one part of the city, like east or west Belfast. Each of the wards had to have at least a 90/10 per cent division according to religion, so making them at least either 90 per cent Catholic or 90 per cent Protestant. In actual fact this was not difficult as much of Northern Ireland is very religiously segregated. As the 1991 Northern Ireland census reveals, about half of the enumeration districts in the whole jurisdiction are actually more than 90 per cent Catholic, or 90 per cent Protestant. As a consequence, a number of the wards selected were up to 99 per cent either Catholic or Protestant, making them almost totally segregated. The wards also had to be in the bottom fifth of the matrix deprivation rank order for Northern Ireland. This made them some of the poorest and socio-economically disadvantaged communities in Northern Ireland and arguably some of the most disadvantaged areas in the whole of the United Kingdom.

In terms of the physical characteristics of the urban lower working-class religiously divided communities, these were areas that were extremely distinctive to the observer. They were most often comprised of poor quality public housing, in the form of large estates. Evidence of decay and social disorder were obvious from the number of empty or derelict and boarded-up houses, the large amounts of graffiti and vandalism and the obvious physical attempts to minimise vandalism, like the widespread use of steel shutters on shop fronts. In some of the areas there were steel grills over the traffic lights to stop them being smashed, and many of the roads, especially around more major junctions, were scarred by the damage caused by burnt-out cars. The extent of sectarian division was also clearly visible for all those living there or passing through to see. This was not only in the sectarian nature of the graffiti, but was evident by the painted kerbstones in red, white and blue, or green, white and gold, as well as the abundance of bunting, sectarian flags, emblems and large political and sectarian murals often carefully painted on the gable ends of houses, all giving a clear message of the intense segregation in these areas.

By contrast, the urban, upper middle-class, religiously mixed communities could not have been more different to the divided lower working-class areas. The three wards selected were in the top fifth of the matrix deprivation rank order, making them some of the most affluent areas in Northern Ireland. They were selected on the basis of religious integration and none of the wards chosen had any more than a 60/40 per cent split according to religion. Their physical characteristics were also striking in that much of the housing was typically large red-brick Victorian, many of which were detached, semi-detached or large terraced properties. They were mostly situated in well established neighbourhoods with mature tree-lined avenues and in well-kept grounds. Evidence of the relative affluence of these areas was clear from the high quality housing, expensive cars parked in driveways, and the well-kept streets and lack of vandalism or graffiti. It was also clear observing these areas that they were not in any way overtly sectarian or religiously divided. Indeed, there were little to no signs of sectarian divisions like graffiti, sectarian flags or painted curb stones. In many respects, they were communities that could have easily been mistaken for some of the most affluent residential areas in Britain.

Away from the large urban area of Belfast, four wards were picked to represent the small-town, religiously divided, lower middle-class communities. The aim was to provide a contrast to the large urban areas and explore the experiences of those living in small-towns and more rural communities. It was originally intended to make these areas directly comparable to the urban, lower working-class divided communities, however, this was just not possible as we were unable to find quite the same combination of extremes of social deprivation and religious segregation in the small-town areas that were so evident in Belfast. As a result, the wards selected had at least an 80/20 per cent religious division, gave a good geographical spread across Northern Ireland and were all outside the commuter belt of Belfast; so as to avoid picking towns that were simply the extended suburbs or commuter areas of Belfast. They were selected so as to be of similar geographical size and housing density and situated in small-towns of approximately the same size and population. The areas picked were also in the lower mid range of the index of relative deprivation for Northern Ireland, making them broadly lower middle-class, small-town and religiously divided communities.

In essence then, the community types selected for inclusion for this survey represent extremes in social, economic and environmental conditions. They are areas selected for their diversity and extremes so as to allow for comparisons to be made between them, and to explore the extent to which widely differing environmental and social conditions impact upon the experiences of those who live in such areas. In no way, however, should the community types chosen for inclusion in this study be seen as the main or only examples of diversity in Northern Ireland, as clearly they are not. Equally, nor should they be considered together as a whole, to represent all the diverse communities that make up Northern Ireland, as they are not. Rather, they should be considered as some of the more extreme examples of urban/rural, religious and socio-economic divisions that exist in Northern Ireland and were picked to explore the experiences of those who live in such differing conditions.

Problems in the Communities

Taking into account the fact that the communities were chosen to be so different in terms of the extent of religious segregation, the degree of socio-economic deprivation, and whether they were in large urban or small-town locations, it was expected that there would be differences in how people saw and experienced the areas in which they lived. Issues of interest included how these differing environmental conditions, such as litter on the street, noisy neighbours and poor street lighting might affect the quality of life, as well as how individuals actually see or view their communities as places to live. Furthermore, it was important for the research to build up a picture, from the respondent's perspective, of how they perceived their communities and the day-to-day experience of the types of problems they encountered. This was to allow for a broader understanding of how other issues may be affected, such as whether and how often people are victimised, and their attitudes towards the police.

The first part of the questionnaire, therefore, focused on a range of problems and issues for the communities and the extent to which they were seen by the respondents as affecting their individual areas. The questions asked covered a whole range of practical problems to more general issues and concerns. The respondents were asked whether they thought these were the types of problems facing their community at that time, and the extent or degree to which they saw them as major problems or difficulties for their areas.

For simplicity, the types of problems can best be summarised under a number of general categories including, very broad social problems, such as unemployment or the general facilities available in their communities for young people. Questions were also asked about the actual physical environment and their perceptions of the quality of the environment, especially the condition of such things as street lighting, housing and the extent to which vandalism is an issue of concern. They were also asked about more general environmental problems such as noise, teenagers making a nuisance of themselves, and uncontrolled dogs in their neighbourhood. Crime and the specific problems it may cause were asked about, as well as the extent to which they saw criminal behaviour like drug dealing occurring in their communities. Finally, the respondents were asked whether they thought harassment, such as sectarian or racial harassment, was taking place and the extent to which it was a problem.

(a)   Broad Social Problems

This category includes broad social issues or problems that may affect the very nature of a community and how it functions. It includes issues such as the levels of unemployment and the lack of facilities for teenagers. The respondents were questioned about these issues and especially the degree to which they saw these problems affecting their areas. Unsurprisingly, there were considerable differences found between the communities in relation to these matters, and to some extent this undoubtedly reflects the diverse conditions across the communities (for example, see Table A4 in Appendix 1 which shows the widely differing socio-economic conditions across the communities). Perhaps unsurprisingly, for example, only 2 per cent of those living in the upper, mixed middle-class urban communities felt that unemployment was a 'big' problem, while in direct contrast, 82 per cent of those from the Catholic lower working-class areas and 45 per cent of those from the Protestant lower working-class areas felt it was a 'big' problem for their areas (see Table 2.2 below). In the small-towns, unemployment was seen as a 'big' problem for 50 per cent of those from the predominately Catholic areas and 18 per cent of those from the predominately Protestant areas. Clearly these figures show the extent to which there are wide variations across the urban and rural divide in relation to concerns about unemployment, but they also suggest a religious dimension to the issue, in that those from the predominately Catholic lower working-class and small-town areas saw this as more of a problem than those from the predominantly Protestant areas.

Table 2.2   Respondents' Views Regarding Broad Social Problems in their Areas *(% that saw problem as 'big')*

'Could you tell me how much of a problem this is in your area at present?'

	Catholic Lower Working Class Urban	Protestant Lower Working Class Urban	Mixed Middle Class Urban	Catholic Small Towns	Protestant Small Towns
Unemployment	82.4	45	2.0	50.2	18.1
Little for teenagers to do	64.2	55.5	18.2	66.1	63.0

(Weighted Data)

One can only speculate why such differences occur. For example, it may be due to real differences in the unemployment rates between the Catholic and Protestant communities. Certainly there is evidence of differential levels of unemployment in Northern Ireland that have disadvantaged Catholics in particular (see Geddis, 1997; Labour Force Survey, 1994). However, this explanation is unlikely for the communities selected in this survey, given they were matched according to relative deprivation which takes into account unemployment rates. A more plausible explanation may be that the differential unemployment rates between Catholics and Protestants may cause some of the differences in the perception of unemployment as a problem: it is seen as more of an issue by Catholic respondents than Protestant respondents. Certainly previous research has shown that Catholic respondents are more likely to see unemployment and discriminatory employment practices as a problem than their Protestant counterparts (Whyte, 1990; Cairns, 1987).

The problem of 'little for teenagers to do' also shows a similar pattern to that experienced in relation to 'unemployment', although the differences between the communities were not so dramatic. Only 18 per cent of those from the mixed middle-class urban areas reported this as a 'big' problem for their area, while over half of all respondents in the other areas thought it was a 'big' problem (see Table 2.2).

It is important to note that these broader social problems were ranked as a 'big' problem by many more respondents than most of the other types of problems which they were questioned about (see below). It appears that many of the communities identified with these issues and saw them as major concerns for their communities - the most noticeable exception being the mixed middle-class urban areas, especially in relation to the question of unemployment. Indeed the importance of broad social problems like unemployment or even little for teenagers to do is mirrored in other national surveys (e.g. British Crime Survey) which place such issues high on the agenda of respondent's concerns. However, significantly, this survey also demonstrates the relevance of community in mediating the nature of such responses.

(b)   Environmental Problems - Living Space Issues

For environmental problems that relate to living space issues the research focused in on the different physical conditions in the communities, especially concerns around poor street lighting, poor housing and other concerns that relate to the physical condition or fabric of the communities. The focus here was on how differing physical conditions within communities can affect how individuals perceive their environment and the problems they have to face living there.

Generally, it was found that very few of those living in the mixed middle-class urban areas saw living space issues such as poor street lighting, poor housing or litter and graffiti as a 'big' problem in comparison to those in the other communities, especially the urban areas. For example, only 6 per cent of those from the upper middle-class mixed communities saw litter and graffiti as a 'big' problem, whereas 30 per cent of those from the Protestant and 46 per cent of those from the Catholic lower working-class areas considered this as a 'big' problem in their areas. Obviously, this reflects to a large extent the better physical conditions in many of the upper middle-class areas. Indeed, higher proportions of respondents in the Protestant and Catholic lower working-class areas reported issues such as poor housing, empty properties, and poor street lighting as a 'big' problem in their communities.

Table 2.3 Respondents' Views Regarding Environmental Problems/ Living Space Issues in their Area *(% that saw problem as 'big')*

'Could you tell me how much of a problem this is in your area at present?'

	Catholic Lower Working Class Urban	Protestant Lower Working Class Urban	Mixed Middle Class Urban	Catholic Small Towns	Protestant Small Towns
Poor street lighting	7.4	7.7	2.1	7.4	5.3
Poor housing	7.8	5.4	0.4	2.6	0.6
Empty properties	5.8	11.5	0.9	1.1	1.0
Poor public transport	6.1	2.0	2.1	13.4	9.7
Litter and graffiti	45.8	29.8	0.6	16.3	15.0
Poor shopping facilities	9.1	21.1	2.6	12.6	20.9

(Weighted Data)

Respondents in the small-town areas generally saw living space issues as less of a problem than those from the urban areas, especially those from the lower working-class areas. However, there were some exceptions and these mostly could be related to the physical isolation of the small-town communities. For example, public transport was more often seen as a 'big' problem in the small-towns than any of the urban areas and poor shopping facilities and poor street lighting were also identified as a big problem in the small-towns (see Table 2.3).

(c)   Environmental Problems - Issues of Disorder

Another set of environmental problems that were considered relate to 'public order' in the communities. These include issues such as, nuisances caused by noise, public drunkenness, uncontrolled dogs, neighbourhood disputes, etc. (see Table 2.4 below). It is evident that many more respondents from the lower working-class areas considered these issues a 'big' problem in their communities. The respondents from these areas appeared to be more concerned by issues of public disorder than those in either the small-town areas or the mixed middle-class urban areas. This is especially true for issues such as nuisances from noise and uncontrolled dogs, or disturbances from teenagers. For instance, some 32 per cent of those from the Catholic and 20 per cent from the Protestant lower working-class communities said poor parental control over children was a 'big problem' in their area. This was in comparison to only 4 per cent of those in the mixed upper middle-class and only 7 and 4 per cent in the Catholic and Protestant small-town areas respectively.

Indeed many of the environmental problems appear to cluster together, especially in the lower working-class urban communities. This may well have been because such problems are often associated with one another, so problems with teenagers may be associated with noise nuisances, under-age drinking and public drunkenness. In effect, many of the differing kinds of problems go together and, when one is evident, it is often associated with many others.

Surprisingly, perhaps, the results show that very few of the respondents across the communities thought parades and demonstrations were a big problem. This may seem odd given the level of public disturbance often associated with parades in Northern Ireland, especially following the Drumcree parade of 1996 and others which occurred around the time of the interviews. However, it may well be that the low numbers reporting such problems is due to the fact that the questions asked were very specific, locating such problems to local areas at that time. No doubt if the questions were asked where some of these controversial parades had occurred, there may have been very different results. Similarly, if the questions had been more generalised, as to whether the respondents felt parades and demonstrations were a big problem in Northern Ireland as a whole, then very different results might have been obtained.

Table 2.4   Respondents' Views Regarding Environmental Problems/Issues of Disorder in their Area (% that saw the problem as 'big')

'Could you tell me how much of a problem this is in your area at present?'

	Catholic Lower Working Class Urban	Protestant Lower Working Class Urban	Mixed Middle Class Urban	Catholic Small Towns	Protestant Small Towns
Nuisance from noise	13.9	9.5	2.6	1.9	4.1
Public drunkenness	22.1	7.5	2.3	10.8	10.6
Uncontrolled dogs	39.1	25.9	17.5	17.9	7.2
Teenager disturbances	13.5	9.5	4.9	3.2	2.6
Poor parental control	32.3	20.1	4.4	7.4	4.0
Underage drinking	43.1	18.6	9.3	40.1	14.5
Parades and demonstrations	2.7	0.0	1.8	0.0	2.2
Neighbourhood disputes	4.4	2.7	0.1	1.8	0.4

(Weighted Data)

(d)   Crime Problems

The questions asked in relation to crime problems in the communities relate directly to a number of specific types of crimes. Similar to many of the other types of problems asked about, the pattern that emerges shows that more of those questioned in the lower working-class areas saw crime as a 'big problem' for their communities. For example, arson, vehicle theft, joyriding and punishment beatings were, on the whole, seen as more of a problem in the lower working-class divided communities than any of the other areas. However, there are some clear exceptions. For example, in the Catholic small-town areas nearly a quarter of respondents reported that drug abuse and drug dealing was a 'big problem'. By comparison, only 8 per cent of those from the Protestant small-towns and less than 1 per cent of those in the mixed middle-class urban areas saw drug abuse or dealing as a 'big problem'. On the other hand, vehicle theft was considered a 'big problem' in the mixed upper middle-class urban areas by about 13 per cent of the respondents. This was higher than any of the other areas, except the Catholic lower working-class communities (30.5 per cent). Generally though, it appeared that more people from the Catholic lower working-class areas than any other areas saw crime as a 'big' problem in their community: drug abuse was seen as such by 24 per cent, vehicle theft by 31 per cent, joyriding by 38 per cent and punishment beatings by 17 per cent (see Table 2.5).

Table 2.5 Respondents' Views Regarding Crime in their Area *(% that saw problem as 'big')*

'Could you tell me how much of a problem this is in your area at present?'

	Catholic Lower Working Class Urban	Protestant Lower Working Class Urban	Mixed Middle Class Urban	Catholic Small Towns	Protestant Small Towns
Drug abuse and dealing	24.4	11.9	0.5	23.0	7.5
Arson	8.5	6.4	1.3	0.0	0.0
Vehicle theft	30.5	10.7	12.6	1.9	0.7
Joyriding	37.7	4.2	1.5	0.6	0.0
Punishment beatings	17.0	1.7	0.1	0.0	0.0

(Weighted Data)

Clearly the results show some areas are much more affected by crime than others. In some communities, certain types of crimes are also perceived to be a real problem. For example, in contrast to the lower working-class urban communities, the small-town areas ranked very few of the crimes as a 'big' problem. However, drug abuse and drug dealing was ranked as a 'big' problem in the Catholic small-town communities. On further analysis it is evident that only one of the Catholic small-town areas generated this finding, which further goes to show the degree to which some specific problems may be highly localised.

(e)   Harassment

The issue of harassment within the context of community problems was also considered and respondents were asked about both racial and sectarian harassment, as well as paramilitary and police harassment. It was found that racial harassment was hardly ever reported to be a 'big' problem in any of the communities. Interestingly, only the Catholic small-town areas even rated it as a problem at all. No doubt this result is due to the generally low numbers of ethnic minorities in Northern Ireland (Northern Ireland Census 1991). Though it must be said that estimating such numbers is difficult given that census questions do not ask about the ethnic background of individuals directly, rather they are based on the religious affiliation of respondents. Other estimates also suggest a very small ethnic minority population in Northern Ireland and the relatively low numbers of such respondents within our sample may well have led to this result. Certainly we would not suggest that racial harassment is not an issue for communities in Northern Ireland (e.g., McVeigh, 1998). It may well be that to properly explore the extent of racial harassment, a more focused survey would be necessary. Such a survey would use boosted samples of those from racial minorities, asking about their experiences and perceptions of harassment.

In relation to other forms of harassment, although the numbers are generally low, it was found that respondents in the lower working-class communities appeared to be exposed to more harassment than those in the middle-class or small-town areas. For example, some 5 per cent and 3 per cent (respectively) of respondents from the Catholic and Protestant lower working-class communities, in comparison to only between 0 and 2 per cent in the other communities, said sectarian harassment was a 'big problem'. In the Protestant lower working-class areas a similar proportion of about 3 per cent of respondents saw sectarian, paramilitary and police harassment in their areas as a big problem. However, in the Catholic lower working-class communities not only did more of the respondents rank harassment as a big problem, but more ranked police harassment as a bigger problem than any of the other forms of harassment asked about. Indeed some 10 per cent saw police harassment as a big problem in the Catholic lower working-class communities in comparison to only between 2 and 0 per cent in the other communities (see Table 2.6).

Table 2.6 Respondents' Views Regarding Harassment in their Area *(% that saw problem as 'big')*

'Could you tell me how much of a problem this is in your area at present?'

	Catholic Lower Working Class Urban	Protestant Lower Working Class Urban	Mixed Middle Class Urban	Catholic Small Towns	Protestant Small Towns
Sectarian harassment	4.7	2.8	1.9	0.0	0.7
Racial harassment	0.0	0.0	0.0	0.7	0.0
Paramilitary harassment	5.4	2.7	0.0	0.3	0.0
Police harassment	10.1	2.2	0.4	0.3	0.0

(Weighted Data)

The Top Five Issues in the Communities

To gain another perspective on the types of problems experienced across the communities the top five problems were ranked as either a 'big' or 'a bit' of a problem for all the communities. From this analysis it can be seen (see Table 2.7) that crime and policing matters were not the most important or major issues for the communities. Rather, more general issues such as unemployment, lack of facilities for teenagers, and other matters such as litter and graffiti, appeared to be of more concern for many of the communities, as discussed above.

A number of particular concerns were also found to be very localised within communities. For example, joyriding was ranked as one of the major problems in the Catholic lower working-class communities. This finding corresponds with recent evidence (McCullough *et al.*, 1990; R.U.C. Chief Constable's Report, 1997) suggesting that these areas may be exposed to considerably higher levels of car theft and joyriding. The results also appear to support the suggestion that some cars may be stolen and brought into the Catholic lower working-class areas, where much of the joyriding actually takes place. This is supported not least by the fact that respondents from the mixed middle-class urban areas saw vehicle theft as one of the major problems in their areas (ranked the second most important problem - see Table 2.7) but they did *not* rank joyriding as a major problem in their area. In other words they felt their cars were being stolen in their areas, but they did not see them being driven around or the joyriding taking place. In comparison those from the Catholic lower working-class communities saw both vehicle theft *and* joyriding as major problems in their communities (see Tables 2.7 and 2.5 above).

Drug abuse and drug dealing is another issue where perceptions widely differed. Both the Protestant and Catholic small towns ranked this as one of the major concerns for their communities. This finding is perhaps somewhat surprising as it is often assumed that drug problems are associated with inner city areas and areas perhaps with high levels of socio-economic deprivation. However this was not found to be the case in relation to the top five problems identified in the communities. It may have been that a number of factors are responsible for this finding. For example, it could be argued that intolerance of drug dealing and possible paramilitary intimidation, especially in the lower working-class divided communities, may have acted to suppress such activities in these particular communities.

Certainly graffiti evident in some of the lower working-class areas, stating that 'drug dealers will be shot', shows marked intolerance towards drugs and drug dealing[1]. However, equally, other local factors may well have played an important role, such as a greater, or lower tolerance in different local areas as well as differences in how these activities are policed and controlled locally. Also, it may well be that, given the smaller range of problems faced by those in the small-town communities (especially in comparison to the lower working-class communities), the issue of drugs ranked higher as one of their concerns.

Overall in relation to the problems faced by individuals living in the differing communities, these findings show how differences between communities - some of which follow expected patterns while others were quite different - are important to those living in them and the extent to which they shape their experiences. Such results also lend a great deal of support to the extent to which local circumstances and conditions do actually differ and how communities are differentially affected by a whole

---

[1] McEvoy *et al.* (1998) argue that there are some distinctions between paramilitary factions with regard to drug dealing and distribution in Northern Ireland. They contend that while both main Loyalist paramilitary factions are involved in drug dealing, as are a number of Republican splinter groups, there is little evidence to suggest that the IRA has been engaged in such activities.

range of problems. Further they show how important it is to locate our understanding of the range of problems people experience as well as their attitudes and opinions, to their social environment and the social conditions in which they find themselves. Without an understanding of the diversity of communities and the wide range of social and environmental conditions between them, it may not be possible to fully understand the sometimes complex array of problems and issues that people face.

Table 2.7   Top Five Issues that People Considered to be a 'Big Problem' or a 'Bit of a Problem' in the Areas at Present

Catholic Lower Working Class Urban	Protestant Lower Working Class Urban	Mixed Middle Class Urban	Catholic Small Towns	Protestant Small Towns
Unemployment 90%	Little for Teenagers to do 76%	Little for teenagers to do 56%	Little for teenagers to do 87%	Little for teenagers to do 81%
Little for teenagers to do 77%	Unemployment 70%	Vehicle theft 53%	Unemployment 74%	Unemployment 42%
Joyriding 62%	Litter and graffiti 61%	Uncontrolled dogs 46%	Underage drinking 59%	Litter and graffiti 41%
Underage drinking 58%	Uncontrolled dogs 54%	Underage drinking 41%	Drugs (including dealing) 49%	Drugs (including dealing) 40%
Poor parental control over children 53%	Underage drinking 45%	Litter and graffiti 41%	Uncontrolled dogs 48%	Poor shopping facilities 39%

Satisfaction with the Communities

Despite such widely differing conditions and the range of problems experienced across the communities, as well as the very differing ways they were perceived by the respondents, over 80 per cent actually reported that they were either 'very' or 'fairly satisfied' with their area. The highest levels of satisfaction were reported in the mixed middle-class urban areas where 96 per cent were either 'very' or 'fairly satisfied' and in the small-town areas where 96 per cent of respondents from the Catholic and 94 per cent of those from the Protestant small-towns were 'very' or 'fairly satisfied'. Both of the lower working-class communities had only a slightly lower proportion of respondents who reported being 'very' or 'fairly' satisfied with the area in which they lived. Indeed, only a small proportion of individuals from these areas were either 'fairly' or 'very dissatisfied' with their area, with 17 per cent in the Catholic and 15 per cent in the Protestant lower working-class areas saying they were either 'fairly' or 'very dissatisfied'.

Further gauging satisfaction with the communities the respondents were also asked how they would feel about moving away from their community. A broadly similar picture emerged here with more of those from the upper middle-class urban areas and the small-town areas saying they would be 'sorry' to move, and between 73 per cent and 68 per cent respectively said they would be 'a bit' or 'very sorry' to move. Only slightly fewer of those from the Catholic and Protestant lower working-class areas (65 per cent and 61 per cent respectively) said that they would be 'a bit' or 'very sorry' to move from their community. Similarly, the same pattern is evident when the respondents were asked if they would 'like' to move, with slightly lower proportions of those from the small-town and middle-class mixed communities expressing a desire to move than those from the lower working-class communities.

Notwithstanding the relatively small differences found between the communities in terms of the general levels of satisfaction, it appears that even though they were very different to each other across a range of indicators, the majority of the respondents reported that they were satisfied with their communities. This finding appears somewhat unusual as it might be expected that those living in some of the most difficult, poorest and most segregated areas would have been the least satisfied. However such a pattern was as clear as it might have been expected and many of those in the most severe and poorest conditions appeared to be quite happy with their community, despite in some cases the multitude of problems associated with them. Thus, it appears that overall satisfaction with an area or community may be related to a wider set of factors than simply the social problems and difficulties experienced within them and many people are relatively satisfied, despite the problems they have to face.

Table 2.8   **Respondents' Views Regarding the Type of Community in which they Live**

'In general what kind of neighbourhood would you say you live in?'

	Catholic Lower Working Class Urban	Protestant Lower Working Class Urban	Mixed Middle Class Urban	Catholic Small Towns	Protestant Small Towns
Help each other	39.9	23.2	19.2	37.7	51.0
Go own way	29.3	44.8	39.9	37.2	34.5
Mixture	30.6	30.4	40.1	24.4	14.2
Don't know	0.1	1.5	0.9	0.7	0.3

(Weighted Data)

It is clear that there were also differences in how much of a sense of community there was in the various areas. The respondents, for example, were asked about the kind of neighbourhood they lived in; whether they thought it was an area where people do things together and try to help each other, or whether it was an area in which people mostly go their own way (see Table 2.1 below). Those from the mixed middle-class areas were least likely to say that their community was an area in which people help each other (19 per cent) followed by the Protestant lower working-class areas (23 per cent). By contrast, many of those from the small-towns and Catholic lower working-class areas reported that they felt people helped each other in their community. Such results appear to suggest that there may be a slightly stronger feeling of 'community spirit' in some communities, which may in some ways help to support or boost satisfaction for people living in these areas.

It is also evident, though, that satisfaction with one's area does not necessarily relate directly to a 'sense of community'. For example, higher levels of satisfaction were noted from those living in the upper mixed middle-class urban areas, despite the fact that they were less likely to have described their community as a place where people help each other. This may be due partly to the fact that many of those respondents from the mixed middle-class areas had not lived in their areas as long as those from the other communities and therefore may not have yet built up as strong community ties. It is also possible, however, that such findings could reflect some of the more subtle differences in the nature of relations between individuals living in very differing communities. So, for some respondents privacy may be an important element in determining their level of satisfaction with their community, while for others a sense of community and satisfaction with it is based on sharing and helping each other, so to help overcome and deal with the many problems they may face.

Conclusions

This chapter shows the importance of community in relation to a whole range of physical, social and environmental conditions, and how they differ between areas - even at a local level. The communities chosen for inclusion in the survey had very obvious and different physical characteristics. For example, in the lower working-class religiously segregated areas there were clear signs of social and economic deprivation, ranging from poor and over-crowded housing, evidence of social decay and vandalism, to inadequate and often run down amenities. Added to this, there were very clear signs of religious segregation and sectarian conflict, from daubed sectarian slogans to carefully painted murals and kerbstones, and sectarian flags and bunting. In contrast, the urban upper middle-class mixed communities were characterised by their affluence, from the large homes, expensive cars, and well-kept gardens, to the lack of any obvious indicators of social decay or religious segregation. The small-towns also provide a contrast in their physical make up, being located in small-town and rural communities and their relative isolation from many of the problems associated with the large urban areas.

The differences evident between the communities in terms of their physical, social end environmental conditions demonstrate the variety and sometimes extremely different conditions that can exist at a community level. Indeed the differences found between the communities is supported by other research, such as that which has been conducted in inner city locations like Islington (Jones *et al.*, 1986; Crawford *et al.*, 1990), Merseyside (Kinsey, 1985), Edinburgh (Anderson *et al.*, 1990) and Dundee (Jones *et al.*, 1994) which has shown the extent to which living conditions and environments differ between areas.

It is also apparent that many of the issues and problems that exist, or are seen to exist, in communities are directly linked into the type of community and local conditions in those areas. Some of the clearest examples of this are found in relation to questions about broad social problems, where for example only 2 per cent of those from the upper middle-class urban areas felt that unemployment was a 'big problem' in their area, while between 45 to 82 per cent of those in the lower working-class areas saw it as a big problem. The very differing conditions evident between communities is also reflected in the responses to questions on the local environment, such as in relation to issues like poor street lighting, litter or graffiti. Those in the lower working-class urban communities reported many more of these environmental and living space issues as real problems for them, in comparison to those living in either the upper middle-class or small-town communities. Such problems extend into issues of disorder, like disturbances from teenagers, public drunkenness and neighbourhood disputes and again it was clear that those living in the lower working-class communities were the most adversely affected. The link between environmental conditions and problems in areas, however, goes beyond a simple class or religious division, as distinct problems emerged for those living in the individual areas. For example, those in the small-towns were more concerned about issues that adversely affect them like poor shopping facilities, the lack of public transport and poor street lighting. Hence showing the link between location and local conditions and the types of problems that people experience.

In relation to the range of problems that people experience, crime was not, generally speaking, the most important issue concerning the respondents, indeed it appeared that the broad social problems like unemployment and lack of activities for teenagers were more often ranked as bigger problems for the communities. Notwithstanding this, it is evident that specific types of crimes were seen as a big problem for some of the communities. For example, car or vehicle theft was a big problem for the upper middle-class areas, while joyriding was of particular concern for the Catholic lower working-class communities. Some of the crime problems were also very localised and the issue of drug dealing provides a good example of this. It was found that concern about drug taking or dealing was especially high in the Catholic small-town areas. However, on further analysis, it was clear that it was just one of the Catholic small-town areas that was responsible for this result, an area where there was an especially high degree of concern about drugs. This emphasises the extent to which some problems are very localised and how they effect areas even on an individual basis.

Not only are many of the problems and issues that people face linked into the type of community they live in, but even relations within communities can differ on a community by community basis. It was found that those in the upper middle-class urban communities were least likely to report that their area was the kind of place where people help each other. On the other hand, those from the small-towns and Catholic lower working-class areas were most likely to say their community was a place where people help each other. The reasons for these differences may be related to a range of factors such as a sense of community spirit, to the desire for privacy, or even the length of time people have been living in a particular area. It shows, though, that relations within communities may be affected by a whole range of issues beyond class, religious division and the urban rural divide.

Despite the extent to which the problems and issues varied between the communities, it was clear, generally speaking, that people were satisfied with the area in which they lived. In fact over 80 per cent of the respondents reported that they were either 'very' or 'fairly' satisfied with the area in which they lived. These findings suggest that broad measures of satisfaction with a community may be related to a wider set of issues than simply the living conditions or problems experienced within them and they may not be the best indicators of the extent to which communities differ in terms of their living conditions. So, while people live in very differing conditions, and are often exposed to a whole array of different problems, they seem to get on and cope with their circumstances.

One of the key elements that emerges from this chapter is the importance of community in terms of how physical and social conditions differ at a local level. Moreover, it shows the way which differing living conditions are often linked into the types of problems people experience at a community level. Since such differences exist at a local level, it is obvious that if one is to attempt to understand the experiences of individuals, then it is necessary to have an understanding of the environment in which they live that takes into account the whole range of differing experiences they may be exposed to. Thus, this chapter in many respects sets the scene for the following chapters which go on to explore a range of experiences and attitudes from crime, victimisation, fear of crime, attitudes towards the police to safety and the use of public space.

3 Crime and Victimisation in the Communities

Introduction

Following on from the perceptions people have of their communities, this chapter seeks to explore the extent to which respondents' experiences of crime may differ, both in terms of suffering and witnessing crime. In particular, it is now possible to test the hypothesis that there are considerable differences in the levels and patterns of victimisation across the various communities. As noted earlier, this idea has been suggested in previous research, where surveys focusing on inner city areas (e.g., Jones *et al.*, 1986; Anderson *et al.*, 1990, Crawford *et al.*, 1990) reveal considerably higher levels of certain types of victimisation in comparison to the levels suggested by national surveys, such as the British Crime Surveys. In contrast, some surveys conducted in rural areas have found considerably lower levels of victimisation, and more recently, British Crime Survey data when broken down by urban and rural areas reveal lower levels of victimisation in rural areas (Mirrlees-Black, 1998). Other surveys which have focused on areas of particular socio-economic disadvantage (e.g., Kinsey, 1984; Jones *et al.*, 1994) have also uncovered higher levels of victimisation in these areas.

To investigate the existence, extent and nature of any such variations within the communities in Northern Ireland, respondents were asked about a range of specific types of victimisation and their experiences of crime in their neighbourhoods. The questions related to crimes which may have been experienced in the twelve months preceding the interview and followed the basic model used in the British Crime Surveys. In other words, the same types of incidents such as burglaries and assaults were asked about, and generally the same types of questions were used concerning these incidents. Unlike the British Crime Surveys, however, specific incidents of victimisation were not explored in detail, but rather the focus was placed upon the number of incidents and how respondents dealt with them.

Ultimately, it is important to caution against making direct comparisons between surveys and reading too much into differences that may emerge. Often differences arise between surveys in terms of their design, implementation and methodologies, so making comparisons problematic. For example, there may be differences in the types of questions asked. Some surveys include a very broad range of incidents while others focus on specific issues or incidents of concern, and these are often related to where the survey is being conducted. For instance, if the survey is in a rural community the types of incidents included may cover a range of questions relating to farms and rural life, and include such things as the theft of livestock and farm machinery. On the other hand, if the survey is conducted in an inner city area questions may focus on issues related to living in a large urban area and the respondent's experiences of city life. Even if the same types of questions are asked, there may also be subtle differences in how they are asked. This can directly effect how the questions are interpreted, which can in turn effect how they are responded to and so produce very differing results. More broadly, there may be differences in the time frame used, for example, whether the incident occurred in the last twelve months, eighteen months, or whether it ever happened in the lifetime of the respondent. There may also be differences in the samples used or in the selection of samples in surveys, whether they are national or local, focusing on the young or elderly, ethnic minorities, or even whether they are focusing on men or women. Indeed, all such factors make direct comparisons between surveys difficult and problematic and should be born in mind when comparisons are made.

Crime and Victimisation

The different types of incidents which the respondents were questioned about are summarised in the following categories:

- Any Type of Crime;
- Household Crime;
- Personal Crime;
- Vehicle Crime; and

- Sectarian Crime.

(a)   Any Type of Crime

The first category of victimisation that was asked about covers all the major types of crime (excluding threats and attempts) that occurred over the previous twelve months. This category gives a good general guide to the extent of victimisation across the communities and allows for very basic comparisons to be made with other recent surveys.

As is evident from Table 3.1, between 25 to 15 per cent of the respondents had been victimised in the previous twelve months. Notwithstanding the problems encountered when comparing survey results, the overall level of victimisation found is lower than that revealed by a number of surveys in other jurisdictions. For example, the British Crime Surveys between 1981 and 1996 found between 28 per cent to 39 per cent of their respondents had been victimised. However, the results from the present survey are similar to the 1995 Northern Ireland Crime Survey results which found a victimisation rate of about 27 per cent over an eighteen month period. Indeed, the results appear to support the view that Northern Ireland has a relatively low level of victimisation, especially if compared to British Crime Survey results. This is further supported by the results of the International Crime Surveys (Mayhew and VanDijk, 1997) of 1989 and 1992 which found that Northern Ireland had a victimisation rate between 12.5 per cent to 15 per cent - one of the lowest rates of the eleven industrialised countries surveyed.

Unlike much of the previous research, this survey also shows how levels of victimisation varied across differing communities. It is evident that urban dwellers, particularly those in the mixed middle-class urban areas are often the most victimised. For example 25 per cent of those in the mixed upper middle-class urban areas and between 22 and 24 per cent of those in the lower working-class areas had been victimised in the previous twelve months. By contrast, only between 15 and 20 per cent of those living in the small towns had been victimised over the same period.

Even though there are differences in the overall levels of victimisation between the communities and indeed the differences are significant statistically, they are not as large as those that have been found in some other local surveys, especially when compared with national survey results (such as the Merseyside or Islington surveys as compared with the British Crime Survey). It appears therefore that the differences in the extent of victimisation across the communities especially between lower working-class and upper middle-class urban communities is not as great in Northern Ireland as has been found in some other jurisdictions. Certainly the differences found were not as large as expected, especially given the fact that the communities chosen were so different to each other in terms of class, location and segregation. It may well be that a number of local and national factors in Northern Ireland are helping to insulate the communities against the worst effects of crime.

Table 3.1   Per Cent of Respondents Victimised by Any Type of Crime in the Previous Twelve Months *(excluding attempts and threats)*

	Catholic Lower Working Class Urban	Protestant Lower Working Class Urban	Mixed Middle Class Urban	Catholic Small Towns	Protestant Small Towns
Any Crime	24.2	21.7	25.0	20.4	14.5

(Weighted Data) Acquisitive crime and vandalism are based on households, violence is based on adults. Risk of any crime is based on adults.

(b)   Household Crime

With regard to this specific form of crime, the main types of household crime considered were burglary, attempted burglary, vandalism and theft from outside the home. In examining the different types of household crime which occurred over the twelve months prior to the interviews, there are a number of general trends that are obvious (see Table 3.2). Generally, less serious offences such as theft outside the home (excluding theft of milk bottles, bicycles or motor vehicles) and vandalism (including vandalism to garden sheds and fences) occurred more frequently with, for example, between 7 to 3 per cent of households experiencing a theft from outside the home in the past twelve months. More serious offences, such as burglary or attempted burglary occurred less frequently: between 1 and 3 per cent of the households in the various communities reported that they had been burgled in the previous twelve months.

Table 3.2   Per Cent of Respondents Victimised by Household Crime in the Previous Twelve Months

	Catholic Lower Working Class Urban	Protestant Lower Working Class Urban	Mixed Middle Class Urban	Catholic Small Towns	Protestant Small Towns
Burglary	1.9	2.8	2.0	1.4	0.3
Attempted burglary	1.9	2.8	2.3	0.7	2.1
Vandalism	2.6	3.8	3.6	3.1	4.1
Theft outside the home	7.1	4.1	5.4	4.9	2.7

(Unweighted Data)

Therefore, it appears that household crime, like many of the other specific forms of victimisation (see below), occurs relatively infrequently across the Northern Irish communities we examined, especially when compared to other national and local surveys in the United Kingdom. While there is evidence that some communities are more often victimised than others, the extent of the differences was slight. For example, those living in the small town communities appear to be less often exposed to household forms of victimisation than those living in the large urban areas and this was especially the case in relation to burglary and attempted burglary. However, vandalism figures were relatively similar across the different communities.

(c)   Personal Crime

The main types of personal crime examined were assault, threats and theft from the person. Within this category assaults and threats occurred more often in all the communities than thefts from the person. However, all of the personal crime categories occurred relatively infrequently, ranging from only 3 per cent of persons assaulted in the Catholic lower working-class areas over the twelve month period, to less than 1 per cent in the Protestant lower working-class areas who were victims of theft from the person (see Table 3.3 below).

Comparing the different communities, there appears to be slightly less personal crime in the small town areas: only 1 per cent reported that they had been assaulted in comparison to between 2 to 3 per cent in the urban areas. However, due to the small numbers, these differences were not statistically significant.

Table 3.3   Per Cent of Respondents Victimised by Personal Crime in the Previous Twelve Months

	Catholic Lower Working Class Urban	Protestant Lower Working Class Urban	Mixed Middle Class Urban	Catholic Small Towns	Protestant Small Towns
Assault	2.7	1.7	1.7	1.4	1.0
Threats	2.1	2.3	1.8	1.4	1.9
Theft from person	0.0	0.8	0.5	1.2	0.4

(Weighted Data)

(d)   Vehicle Crime

Vehicle crime includes bicycle theft, theft of vehicles, theft from a vehicle, and vandalism of a vehicle. These questions were asked only of those who owned a vehicle or bicycle. In general it was found that vehicle vandalism and bicycle theft were reported slightly more frequently than either theft from a vehicle or theft of a vehicle.

Comparing the communities by the differing types of vehicle crime, the low numbers of those victimised meant that many of the differences were not significant. However, vandalism of vehicles was found to be significantly different across the communities (see Table 3.4). It is evident that there were more incidents of vandalism in the urban areas, especially the Catholic lower working-class areas (17 per cent) and Protestant lower working-class areas (11.5 per cent), than the small town areas (5 per cent each for the Catholic and Protestant areas). Also, for theft from a vehicle, it was found that those in the upper middle-class areas were in fact more often victimised than either those in the lower working-class communities or those in the small town areas.

Interestingly, the actual levels of victimisation in relation to theft of vehicles was found to be very different to the extent to which they were seen as a 'big problem' in the communities (as reported in chapter 2). In fact, despite nearly a third (31 per cent) of the respondents from the Catholic lower working-class areas reporting this as a 'big problem' in comparison to only 11 per cent in the Protestant lower working-class areas, the actual victimisation rates across the communities were found to be the same.

Such findings show the extent to which the perception of problems is sometimes not precisely connected to the actual extent of the problems. Rather, such perceptions seem to be more related to how communities view problems and the ways these concerns are communicated within communities. Such results may also be important in relation to the significance of keeping communities correctly informed of the actual levels of crime and victimisation. This approach might also clarify the real risks of crime, so ensuring that people are better informed and as a result possibly less worried.

Table 3.4   Per Cent of Respondents Victimised by Vehicle Crime in the Previous Twelve Months *(only applies to respondents with vehicles)*

	Catholic Lower Working Class Urban	Protestant Lower Working Class Urban	Mixed Middle Class Urban	Catholic Small Towns	Protestant Small Towns
Bicycle theft	12.3	6.3	6.1	2.7	5.2
Vehicle theft	4.7	4.7	3.6	2.1	0.9
Theft from vehicle	4.1	6.8	9.0	3.0	4.7
Vehicle vandalism	16.6	11.5	8.7	4.7	4.7

(Unweighted Data)

(e)   *Sectarian Crime*

Because of the circumstances in Northern Ireland, a range of incidents were asked about which were sectarian in nature. These were incidents which the respondents felt occurred directly because of their religion. These included sectarian verbal abuse, threats, physical attacks and damage to the home.

Generally, the more serious sectarian crimes, especially those of physical attacks and damage to the home, appeared to occur relatively infrequently. Threats and verbal abuse which were identified as sectarian in nature occurred slightly more frequently (see Table 3.5). Unsurprisingly perhaps, the small towns had lower levels of victimisation than the urban areas, especially for sectarian physical attacks and damage to the home. However, given the very low numbers involved, such differences were not found to be statistically significant between communities.

Interestingly, one type of sectarian victimisation that did show a significant difference between the communities was that of verbal abuse. It was found that those from the mixed upper middle-class communities were more likely to have experienced sectarian verbal abuse than individuals from any of the other community types. An explanation for this result is not obvious from the data. However, it may be that living in a religiously mixed area could have increased the possibility of sectarian verbal abuse from others (who were not of the same religion) living in such communities. This could also account for some of the lower levels of such abuse in those communities that were starkly religiously divided. So, in other words, people living in divided communities may be less exposed to sectarian verbal abuse because there are so few people of the other religion there to abuse them. Equally, it may be that the higher reported levels of such abuse in the upper middle-class mixed communities could be related to a lower tolerance of those living in such areas to this type of abuse. Therefore, those in the mixed upper middle-class areas may have been more willing to report such incidents than those in the lower working-class communities. Either way, such results show how crime of a sectarian nature is yet another issue that people in Northern Ireland have to deal with above and beyond 'ordinary' crime.

Overall, the results of this survey in relation to victimisation show how it is spread very unevenly. Like other surveys, both local (e.g., Bottoms *et al.*, 1987; Crawford *et al.*, 1990; and Anderson *et al.*, 1990) and national (e.g., The British Crime Surveys and Northern Ireland Crime Survey, 1996) it shows differences in the risks and extent of victimisation according to the type of incident. For example it was found that there is less risk of incidents against the person, such as assaults, than incidents of property crime such as theft from a vehicle. It also shows that the victimisation rates in the communities examined are generally low. This supports findings that have shown Northern Ireland to be a relatively low crime area especially in comparison to other similar jurisdictions (Mayhew and VanDijk, 1997; Northern Ireland Crime Survey, 1996).

Table 3.5   **Respondents Victimised by Sectarian Crime in the Previous Twelve Months**

	Catholic Lower Working Class Urban	Protestant Lower Working Class Urban	Mixed Middle Class Urban	Catholic Small Towns	Protestant Small Towns
Sectarian verbal abuse	1.0	3.0	5.5	2.3	1.8
Sectarian threats	0.6	1.5	1.3	0.3	0.4
Sectarian attacks	0.8	0.5	0.7	0.0	0.0
Sectarian home damaged	1.0	0.0	0.5	0.3	0.0

(Weighted Data)

In relation to differences found between the communities, while there were differences in the overall levels of victimisation, especially between the small town communities and the urban areas, some of the differences were smaller than expected. This was notable especially given the sharp religious, geographic and socio-economic differences that exist between the communities included in the survey. This finding is also different from much of the previous research which has shown how some areas may be particularly prone to victimisation, especially areas of severe social and economic deprivation. For example, the Dundee surveys (Jones *et al.*, 1991; 1994), which examined a number of lower working-class council estates, found the burglary rate to be around three times the national average, with 5 per cent of households having been burgled in the previous twelve months, according to the 1994 results. The Edinburgh Crime Survey (Anderson *et al.*, 1990) also notes considerably higher levels of particular types of crime in a number of the inner city areas they sampled. It appears that not only was the overall victimisation rate relatively low, but the communities in some ways appeared to be more insulated from crime. Even within the lower working-class communities (where one may have expected to find more victimisation), the levels were actually found to be relatively low.

Reporting Crime to the Police

Those who had been victimised were also asked whether they had reported the incident to the police. These questions were broadened to include those who had *ever* been victimised (rather than only those who been victims in the past twelve months) in order to increase the number of respondents. The same categories of crime are used as in the previous sections.

Reporting Household Crime

More serious forms of household crime, such as burglary and attempted burglary, produced higher levels of reporting to the police. Offences such as vandalism to the home and theft from outside the home generally had lower reporting rates. This appears to follow the trend evident in many other crime surveys where serious offences are more often reported to the police (e.g., Mayhew *et al.*, 1993).

Table 3.6 Per Cent of Respondents Reporting Household Victimisation to the Police *(respondents who had ever been a victim)*

	Catholic Lower Working Class Urban	Protestant Lower Working Class Urban	Mixed Middle Class Urban	Catholic Small Towns	Protestant Small Towns
Burglary	67.7 (23)	93.3 (42)	96.8 (90)	88.0 (22)	94.4 (17)
Attempted burglary	52.9 (9)	50.0 (12)	69.2 (27)	33.3 (2)	50.0 (6)
Vandalism	35.3 (6)	26.1 (6)	47.4 (18)	27.3 (3)	27.8 (5)
Theft outside home	15.6 (10)	24.0 (6)	44.1 (30)	27.9 (12)	28.0 (7)

(Weighted Data) Figures in Tables 3.6 to 3.9 only include individuals who had been victimised *and* reported the incident to the police. Actual numbers are contained in brackets.

No doubt this is related to a number of factors such as the need to report the incident to the police for insurance purposes, the expectations of the victim in terms of whether they feel the police can effectively deal with the matter, and maybe even the relationship between the victim and offender in certain circumstances (e.g., British Crime Survey, 1994).

It is also clear from the results, however, that reporting rates for household crime differ across the community types (see Tables 3.6). The most obvious variation is the considerably lower reporting rate found in the Catholic lower working-class communities, especially with respect to burglary, where only 68 per cent of incidents were reported to the police in comparison to between 88 to 97 per cent in the other communities. Indeed many of the household crimes in the Catholic lower working-class communities appeared to have been less often reported than those from the other communities (although a degree of caution is advised when comparing incidents that occurred relatively infrequently such as vandalism).

Reporting Personal Crime

Reporting rates for personal crime also varied according to both the type of offence and the type of community. However, due to the low number of individuals who were actually victimised, very few of the differences found are statistically significant.

Table 3.7   **Per Cent of Respondents Reporting Personal Crime** *(respondents who had ever been victims)*

	Catholic Lower Working Class Urban	Protestant Lower Working Class Urban	Mixed Middle Class Urban	Catholic Small Towns	Protestant Small Towns
Assault	72.0 (18)	59.6 (34)	57.4 (58)	52.6 (10)	74.2 (23)
Threats	23.1 (6)	46.2 (12)	75.0 (48)	78.9 (15)	58.6 (17)
Theft from person	100 (4)	23.1 (3)	54.1 (20)	39.1 (9)	14.3 (1)

(Weighted Data)

Only 'threats' were found to be significantly different across the community types with as little as 23 per cent of those from the Catholic lower working-class communities reporting threats to the police in comparison to between 46 and 79 per cent in the other communities (see Table 3.7).

Reporting Vehicle Crime

In the case of vehicle crime, there were also differences in reporting rates according to the type of vehicle crime (see Table 3.8). Theft of a vehicle was the most frequently reported to the police, with all such incidents reported in the small towns and Protestant lower working-class communities. On the other hand, vandalism was one of the least reported vehicle crimes with only 26 to 60 per cent being reported to the police across the communities. Again, broad differences in reporting rates between differing types of vehicle crime appear to correspond to their relative seriousness and, as has been previously documented, high reporting rates also may be related to other factors such as the need to report to the police for insurance claims or other such considerations.

Table 3.8   Per Cent of Respondents Reporting Vehicle Crime *(respondents who had ever been victims)*

	Catholic Lower Working Class Urban	Protestant Lower Working Class Urban	Mixed Middle Class Urban	Catholic Small Towns	Protestant Small Towns
Bicycle theft	14.3 (3)	68.4 (13)	79.1 (34)	52.6 (10)	58.8 (10)
Vehicle theft	88.9 (24)	100 (34)	99.0 (97)	100 (18)	100 (16)
Theft from vehicle	43.8 (7)	67.9 (19)	69.9 (65)	75.0 (15)	60.9 (14)
Vehicle vandalism	35.1 (13)	25.8 (8)	60.2 (50)	44.4 (12)	37.0 (10)

(Unweighted Data)

Because of the low numbers, very few of the differences found in reporting vehicle crime between the community types are statistically significant, apart from those in relation to bicycle theft. In relation to this crime, the Catholic lower working-class communities again were far less likely to report such a crime to the police than individuals from any of the other communities. Only 14 per cent of those from the Catholic lower working-class areas actually said they reported the theft of a bicycle to the police, compared to between 53 to 79 per cent of those in the other communities.

Reporting Sectarian Crime

In relation to sectarian crime, since only a small number of respondents were victimised by such incidents, few of the differences uncovered were found to be significant. However, as with the other categories of crime, it appeared that when the crime was more serious, such as sectarian attacks or damage to the home, the rate of reporting to the police was greater than in respect of less serious incidents such as sectarian verbal abuse or threats (see Table 3.9). For example, between 80 to 50 per cent of sectarian incidents involving damage to the home were reported, while less than 15 per cent reported sectarian verbal abuse to the police. Indeed the only category which was found to be significantly different, in a statistical way, across the community types was that of sectarian verbal abuse (yet the numbers were still very small). Those from the Protestant small town areas and mixed middle-class areas appeared to be more likely to report the incident to the police than individuals from the other communities.

Table 3.9   Per Cent of Respondents Reporting Sectarian Crime *(respondents who had ever been victims)*

	Catholic Lower Working Class Urban	Protestant Lower Working Class Urban	Mixed Middle Class Urban	Catholic Small Towns	Protestant Small Towns
Sectarian Verbal Abuse	5.7 (2)	3.9 (2)	9.6 (13)	0.0 (0)	14.8 (8)
Sectarian Threats	21.2 (7)	13.5 (5)	24.6 (17)	0.0 (0)	18.2 (2)
Sectarian Attacks	34.5 (10)	27.8 (5)	25.0 (11)	0.0 (0)	0.0 (0)
Sectarian Home Damage	80.0 (8)	50.0 (2)	80.0 (12)	50.0 (1)	50.0 (1)

(Weighted Data)

Reasons For Not Reporting Incidents to the Police

Respondents who said that they had been victimised but had not reported the incident to the police were asked what was the main reason for not reporting the offence. Although the numbers are relatively small, it is evident that there are a number of clearly different reasons for not reporting. As in other surveys, one of the major reasons for not reporting is because the respondent felt the incident was 'too trivial' or 'not worth reporting'; between 55 to 22 per cent of those who had been victimised but did not report the incident gave this as the reason. Other major reasons given included the feeling by respondents that the police could do nothing about it, or that they themselves would deal with the incident. Similar to British Crime Survey results (Mayhew *et al.*, 1993), few (less than 8 per cent across the communities) said they did not report the incident because they feared or disliked the police.

However, it is also clear that there were different reasons given for not reporting crime to the police across the community types. For instance, those from the Catholic small towns and the mixed middle-class areas were most likely to say the incident was too trivial or not worth reporting (55 and 48 per cent respectively gave this as their main reason for not reporting the offence, see Table 3.10). By comparison, only 22 to 30 per cent of those from the Catholic and Protestant lower working-class communities respectively said it was too trivial or not worth reporting.

It is evident that respondents from the Catholic lower working-class areas differed to those in the other community types with respect to the reasons they gave for not reporting incidents to the police. Indeed, 31 per cent of respondents from the Catholic lower working-class communities said that they felt the incident was either a 'private or personal matter', or they would deal with it themselves, as compared with only between 9 to 12 per cent of those from the other communities.

For those from the small town communities, it was clear that they were most likely to focus on offence-related factors for not reporting incidents to the police, like the incident being too trivial or not worth reporting. For those in the urban areas there was also a significant proportion who related their reasons to offence-related factors, but they were also more likely to cite police related reasons, such as the view that the police could do nothing about the incident. This was especially true of those from the Protestant lower working-class (41 per cent) and mixed upper middle-class areas (24 per cent). The respondents from the Catholic lower working-class communities, on the other hand, were less likely to say the incident was too trivial or not worth reporting and most likely to say they would deal with the matter themselves, or they felt it was a private or personal matter.

Table 3.10 Main Reason for Not Reporting Incident to the Police *(per cent of respondents who had ever been victims)*

	Catholic Lower Working Class Urban	Protestant Lower Working Class Urban	Mixed Middle Class Urban	Catholic Small Towns	Protestant Small Towns
Private, personal or family matter	18.2	0.4	2.2	5.9	3.8
Dealt with it myself	14.9	9.3	6.9	5.9	8.2
Reported to Republican /Loyalist group	0.0	0.0	0.2	0.0	0.0
Dislike/fear of police	8.2	0.4	0.0	0.0	0.0
Fear of reprisal by offenders	4.8	2.2	2.2	2.0	1.3
Police could do nothing	5.2	41.2	23.7	6.9	17.1
Police would not have bothered /not interested	7.8	5.3	2.5	1.0	4.4
Inconvenient/too much trouble	11.5	0.9	0.2	3.4	4.4
No loss/damage	0.0	3.1	3.0	1.0	3.2
Attempt at offence unsuccessful	0.0	3.1	2.7	0.5	1.3
Did not want to attract attention by having police here	6.7	0.0	3.0	5.4	4.4
Too trivial/not worth reporting	21.9	30.1	48.4	55.4	40.5
Other	0.7	4.0	4.9	12.7	11.4

(Weighted Data)

Moreover, those from the Catholic lower working-class areas were more likely to say they disliked the police, that they did not want to attract attention by having the police in their area, or that the police would not have bothered, it was inconvenient, or it was too much trouble to report the incident to the police.

To some extent the differing reasons given for not reporting incidents to the police probably relate to the differing patterns of victimisation found across the communities. However, they also appear to reflect the differing experiences of policing and differing attitudes towards the police which can be found across Northern Ireland (e.g., PANI, 1996; O'Mahony and Quinn, 2000). More generally, however, the results show the importance of considering local dimensions in exploring the experiences and attitudes of respondents and their motivations for reporting or not reporting to the police as they differ so considerably at a community level (see chapter five on policing for a fuller discussion).

Witnessing Crime

Lastly, as another way of looking at differences between the various communities with respect to crime and victimisation, the respondents were asked if they had actually seen or witnessed any of a number of incidents occurring in their community over the past three years. The questions focus on a number of particular types of crime and were asked only of those respondents who had lived in their area for three years or more and therefore could be assumed to have firm roots within the individual communities.

There are a number of general patterns with respect to witnessing crime that are evident from the respondents in the communities. Acts such as vandalism and serious fights were some of the most commonly witnessed incidents, with between 22 to 8 per cent of the respondents saying they had witnessed acts of vandalism and between 18 to 10 per cent saying they had seen a serious fight in their area. On the other hand, some incidents were witnessed considerably less often, with only between 1 to 16 per cent saying they had witnessed someone steeling from a car in their area (see Table 3.11). There were also notable differences between the communities in the number of respondents that had witnessed events occurring in their areas. In general though, it was found that more respondents from the Catholic lower working-class communities had witnessed the incidents that were asked about than those from the other areas.

One of the most striking findings, in relation to differences between the communities, concerned joyriding. It was found that as much as 58 per cent of those from the Catholic lower working-class communities had witnessed joyriding in their community. By comparison, only between 10 to less than 1 per cent of those in the other communities had witnessed joyriding. Certainly this was the most dramatic difference between the areas and demonstrates vividly (as highlighted earlier) how communities may be differentially exposed to specific problems and incidents in their areas.

Table 3.11 Per Cent of Respondents Witnessing Crime in their Areas over the Past Three Years

	Catholic Lower Working Class Urban	Protestant Lower Working Class Urban	Mixed Middle Class Urban	Catholic Small Towns	Protestant Small Towns
Vandalism	22.3	19.7	14.3	12.0	8.4
Drug abuse and drug dealing	13.9	5.5	6.0	11.3	7.8
Joyriding	58.0	9.7	6.4	4.5	0.6
Serious fight	19.3	11.1	10.3	17.6	9.6
Theft from a vehicle	15.6	3.7	4.4	1.0	0.5

(Weighted Data)

The witnessing of drug abuse or drug dealing also produced some interesting findings. It was found that 11 per cent of those from the Catholic small towns, and 14 per cent of those from the Catholic lower working-class communities, said they had witnessed drug abuse or drug dealing in their communities. This was in contrast to only between 6 and 8 per cent of those in the other communities. Indeed only 6 per cent of those in the Protestant lower working-class areas said they had seen such activities, which was actually the lowest proportion of all the community types (see Table 3.11). Hence, the pattern of witnessing events was not always straightforward nor simply concentrated in the lower working-class areas.

Moreover, it was found that the pattern of witnessing events was not even consistent within some of the community types. It was found, for example, that 11 per cent of respondents from the Catholic small towns had witnessed drug dealing or drug taking, which appeared surprisingly high. In fact, on further analysis, it was found that just one of the Catholic small town areas accounted for the higher than expected result (as noted in chapter two with respect to crime problems). These findings again demonstrate the extent to which some problems are very localised, even within community types.

Reporting Witnessed Crime

Respondents who had witnessed incidents in their communities in the previous three years were further asked whether or not they had reported them to the police. Generally, it was found that the reporting rates were lower for incidents that respondents had witnessed in comparison to incidents they had either experienced personally, or which had involved their household (as discussed earlier). There were also some differences in reporting according to the type of incident and community type. However, due to the low numbers that had witnessed events, only some of the differences in reporting rates between the communities were actually significant in a statistical sense. In particular, there were significant differences found across the communities in those witnessing vandalism or a serious fight and those who were willing to report. Those from the mixed middle-class and Protestant small towns were more inclined to report such incidents to the police than those from the other community types (see Table 3.12). For the differing types of incidents witnessed, it was found that witnessing theft from a vehicle was most likely to result in the incident being reported, with between 36 per cent to all such incidents being reported across the communities (see Table 3.12). Conversely, and somewhat surprisingly, given the level of concern expressed earlier, witnessing drug abuse and drug dealing was in fact one of the least likely events to be reported to the police, with only 14 to 21 per cent being reported.

Table 3.12 Per Cent of Respondents who had Witnessed Crime and Reported it to the Police *(over the previous three years)*

	Catholic Lower Working Class Urban	Protestant Lower Working Class Urban	Mixed Middle Class Urban	Catholic Small Towns	Protestant Small Towns
Vandalism	17.3	18.8	38.5	16.9	40.7
Drug abuse or drug dealing	14.4	16.1	10.0	20.5	14.0
Joyriding	24.9	23.6	26.6	25.8	0.0
Serious fight	23.7	1.6	34.0	18.0	32.3
Theft from a vehicle	35.8	33.3	61.4	85.7	100

(Weighted Data)

Conclusions

In relation to crime and victimisation, this chapter shows the overall levels of victimisation across the communities were relatively low. Only between 15 to 25 per cent of the respondents had been victimised by 'any crime' in the past twelve months. This finding corresponds to other recent research which has shown relatively low levels of crime in Northern Ireland - despite the political conflict or 'troubles'. For example, the Northern Ireland Crime Survey (1995) found a lower level of victimisation than recent crime surveys have found in England and Wales (British Crime Survey results 1998). The International Victimisation Survey (Mayhew and Van Dijk, 1997) also found that Northern Ireland had one of the lowest victimisation rates of the eleven industrialised countries surveyed and successive figures on recorded crime provided by the police and Northern Ireland Office show a comparatively low overall crime rate (Royal Ulster Constabulary, 1998; Northern Ireland Office, 1997).

The pattern of victimisation evident from this survey according to offence type also follows that found in other victimisation surveys (e.g., Crawford, 1990; Mirrlees-Black *et al.*, 1998) with, in general, more incidents of victimisation for less serious types of crimes. So, for offences like vehicle vandalism, it was found that as much as 17 per cent of the respondents were victimised, while for more serious offences, like personal assaults, only between 1 to 3 per cent of the respondents had been victimised over the same period.

The survey results confirmed different rates and patterns of victimisation across the communities. This was especially true between the urban and small town communities and the results supported other research that has found generally lower levels of victimisation in more rural and small town locations, especially in comparison to urban and national results (e.g., Koffman, 1996; Mirrlees-Black, 1998). While the overall levels of victimisation in the small towns was only between 14 and 20 per cent of respondents, the figures for the urban communities was found to be as high as 22 and 25 per cent. Not only was there less crime in the small town areas in general, but there were also differences in the types of victimisation found across the communities. For example, crime relating to vehicles was much more concentrated in the urban areas than small towns. So, vehicle crimes such as theft of a vehicle ranged from 5 to 4 per cent in the urban communities, while it was only between 1 to 2 per cent in the small town areas.

The overall rates of victimisation did not, however, exactly follow the expected patterns in the urban areas. It was anticipated that there would be considerably higher levels of victimisation in the lower working-class communities, especially in comparison to the upper middle-class areas. In fact this was not found to be the case; the upper middle-class areas actually had the highest levels of overall victimisation at 25 per cent, followed closely by the lower working-class areas at 22 and 24 per cent (for the Protestant and Catholic areas respectively). Certainly this is different to much of the previous research in other jurisdictions which show considerably higher levels of victimisation in some inner city areas and in areas with high levels of socio-economic deprivation (e.g., Jones et al., 1991; 1994; Anderson et al., 1990). However, this is not to suggest that inner city areas did not suffer from considerably higher levels of some types of crime. Indeed, the lower working-class communities appeared to be exposed to more vehicle-related offences, such as theft of vehicles and vehicle vandalism, as well as other offences such as threats. Furthermore, considerably more people living in these areas also reported witnessing crimes. Accounting for such differences is difficult, but it may well be that since there was a generally low level of victimisation found across the communities, as evidenced in other research (e.g., Mayhew and VanDijk, 1997; Boyle and Haire, 1996; RUC, 1997), there may be some factors in Northern Ireland which help insulate communities against more widespread crime. Nonetheless, the survey also shows that some people, albeit a very small minority, also had to endure a range of crimes that were sectarian in nature; indeed sectarian motivated crime is another issue which people in Northern Ireland have to deal with.

As previous research has illustrated (Skogan 1990; Bucke 1997), it was found that there were differences in reporting to the police according to the nature of the crime. More serious crimes such as burglary and assaults appeared to be reported more often than minor incidents, e.g., vandalism or thefts outside the home, and vehicle theft was found to be the incident most often reported. There were also differences between the communities in the extent to which incidents were reported to the police. For example (though the numbers were small), it is evident that while those in the Catholic lower working-class communities were victimised more, they were actually less likely to report such incidents to the police. Surprisingly perhaps, even for relatively serious offences like burglary, only 68 per cent of those from the Catholic lower working-class communities reported such incidents to the police, in contrast to between 97 to 88 per cent of those in the other areas.

Not only were there differences in the reporting rates across the communities, there were also differences found in the reasons for not reporting incidents to the police. The most common reasons for not reporting were because the victim felt that the incident was too trivial or not worth reporting, or they felt the police could do nothing about it. However, those in the Catholic lower working-class areas were more likely to say it was a private or personal matter, or that they did not involve the police because they would deal with it themselves. Indeed 31 per cent of those in the Catholic lower working-class areas said it was a private or personal matter, or that they would deal with it themselves, in comparison to only between 9 to 12 per cent of those from the other communities. Though only a small minority of respondents said they feared or disliked the police, the findings suggest that respondents from some communities are far less willing to involve the police when they are victimised. While such a difference may be partly related to differing patterns of victimisation across the communities, it also shows in a more fundamental way that variances in attitudes towards the police occur at a local level, especially in those who did not want to attract attention by having the police in their area, felt the police would not have bothered, or disliked or feared the police.

Clear differences were also found between the communities in terms of witnessing events in their areas. One of the more dramatic differences was that of joyriding. As many as 58 per cent of those from the Catholic lower working-class communities had witnessed joyriding in their community in the previous three years, in comparison to only between 1 to 10 per cent of those from the other communities. Such findings again demonstrate how some types of crime may be very localised and concentrated in individual communities or localities.

Thus, results from this chapter build upon those of the previous chapter which examined the problems and perceptions of the communities and they further show the importance of community in relation to crime and victimisation. These results clearly show the extent to which certain types of victimisation are very localised. It is also apparent that not only is one's experience of crime effected by where the individual lives and their community, but how crime is responded to and whether the police are involved also differs on a community-by-community basis. Hence, in relation to crime and victimisation, this chapter further sets in context the importance of locating individuals in their communities and in understanding the impact of local factors on the distribution and response to crime and victimisation.

4 Worries and Fears in the Communities

Introduction

Above and beyond the day to day problems that respondents have to deal with across the communities, this chapter explores their worries and fears in relation to crime and victimisation. The issues raised illustrate that fear of crime can have a significant impact on the everyday lives of individuals and can transform the overall quality of life in communities (Box *et al.*, 1988). Fear of crime and victimisation may lead some people to change their behaviour, for example, staying indoors at night or avoiding areas that they feel could be dangerous. Some surround themselves with crime prevention devices such as extra locks, doorchains, to security devices on windows. Some people may even start to carry personal alarms (Hale, 1996). Consequently, as Box *et al.* (1988) suggests, fear of crime effects not only quality of life for individuals and communities, but has in and of itself become a major social issue.

The link between fear of crime and communities is important as fears are not only linked to who the individuals are and their characteristics, such as their age and sex, but where they live and the environment in which they find themselves. Research has shown that differing groups of individuals may express differing levels of fear (e.g., Hough, 1995; Mirrlees-Black and Allen, 1998). The young are often less fearful than the elderly, and men often express less fear than women. These findings are relatively consistent, despite differences in victimisation rates which show that women and the elderly are actually less prone to many forms of crime than young males.

It has been suggested, however, that such fears may be a better reflection of an individual's sense of vulnerability rather than their statistical risk of victimisation. So, despite the fact that young males are more likely to be victimised, they tend to express less worries because they feel less vulnerable than women or the elderly. Research also shows that fears are related to local, environmental and community factors, so fears may be related to particular places, be they dark alleys or places with a bad reputation. Often fears are very different in large inner city areas in comparison to small rural communities. As the 1996 British Crime Survey (Mirrless-Black, 1998) shows, people living in rural areas are far less concerned about crime than those in urban areas and they appear to feel safer on their local streets.

Therefore, the emphasis in this chapter is on locating fears and worries in the context of the environment with a view to providing another perspective on issues affecting the quality of life for people living in very different types of communities. Furthermore, the chapter provides an opportunity to look at the differential impact of individual factors, such as age and sex, and community factors on fear of crime and the extent to which community issues like social disorganisation (Shaw and McKay, 1942) may be important in explaining or accounting for such fears.

The chapter starts with an examination of the general fears and worries people experience, and moves on to their worries about specific incidents such as household and personal crime. Finally, it considers how respondents assess the extent of crime in their communities in comparison to the rest of Northern Ireland, Great Britain and the Republic of Ireland, and whether they perceived a change in the levels of crime during the paramilitary cease-fire of 1996.

General Fear of Crime

The first set of questions asked of the respondents relates to their general feelings of safety. These questions were drafted taking into account criticisms (e.g., Garofalo, 1979; Box *et al.*, 1988) which have suggested that some types of questions may be too general in their wording to allow for meaningful analysis in relation to fear of crime. For example, questions that simply ask 'how safe do you feel being out alone at night?' may well be interpreted by the respondent to relate to a whole range of possible issues. These could range from the fear of being mugged, falling down on poorly lit streets, stepping on dog dirt, to even being frightened by shadows. Hence, the questions in this survey were introduced with a general statement to ensure that the respondents knew that they were being asked about fear of crime and that they were being asked to focus on their own community, so locating the fear to their specific environment. The first questions related to how safe people felt in regard to ordinary crime when walking alone in their community, whether during the day or at night. Following on from this, they were asked how safe they felt when they were home alone at night.

In relation to how safe people felt in regard to ordinary crime during the day, the majority of respondents said that they felt either 'very safe' or 'safe' in their communities. In fact, as can be seen from Table 4.1, over 90 per cent of the respondents from the different communities said they felt 'safe' or 'very safe'. There are a number of significant differences, however, between the communities. Between 92 and 89 per cent of those from the small town communities said they felt 'very safe' during the day, whilst only 62 to 77 per cent of those from the large urban communities felt very safe. Clearly, those from the small town communities were more likely to feel 'very safe' than those from the urban areas. Also, within the urban areas it is apparent that those from the Catholic lower working class communities were slightly more likely to say they felt 'a bit unsafe' or 'very unsafe' (9 per cent) than either those from the Protestant lower working class areas (2 per cent) or mixed upper middle class areas (5 per cent).

As might be expected, reported feelings of safety were lowest at night, with only 72 to 88 per cent of respondents saying they felt 'very safe' or 'safe' from crime while walking around their neighbourhoods. Nonetheless, the same general pattern is still evident between the communities with higher proportions of those from the small town areas (between 88 and 81 per cent) reporting that they felt 'very safe' walking alone in their communities at night than those in the urban areas (only between 68 and 73 per cent).

The responses of men and women in the communities were compared and, as with many other surveys (ie.g., Hough, 1995; Boyle and Haire, 1996; Mirrlees-Black and Allen, 1998), women were found to be more likely to report feeling unsafe than men, with this difference being greatest at night-time. In fact, 15 to 20 per cent of the women interviewed felt 'a bit unsafe' or 'very unsafe' at night in comparison to only 7 to 11 per cent of men in the small town communities. Similarly, in the urban communities, 33 to 38 per cent of the women interviewed said that they felt 'a bit unsafe' or 'very unsafe' at night in comparison to only 17 to 21 per cent of the men.

Somewhat unexpectedly, it was clear from the results that general feelings of safety between some of the communities (especially the urban areas) were not as different as they might have been given their very different environmental and social conditions. For instance, it was not found that those from the Catholic and Protestant lower working class communities felt a lot less safe than those in the mixed upper middle class communities. Indeed, some 27 per cent of those from both the Catholic and Protestant lower working class areas said they felt 'a bit unsafe' or 'very unsafe' in their areas at night, in comparison to 26 per cent of those from the mixed upper middle class areas. This is despite earlier findings which showed the very differing conditions and problems in these respective communities, whereby those in the lower working class areas reported many more problems in their areas than those in the upper middle class areas.

It is difficult to assess why those in the lower working class communities did not report higher levels of worry than those in the upper middle class communities, but it may well be that feelings of safety are directly related to factors such as general levels of satisfaction with a community (as reported in chapter two) rather than the differing conditions and problems experienced within them. In fact, as previously noted, the general levels of satisfaction were actually very similar between the urban lower working and upper middle class communities, even though they had very different environmental and social problems (see chapter two). Such findings lend support to research by Hartnagel (1979) which suggests that satisfaction with one's neighbourhood is closely associated with fear of crime. In other words, those people who are satisfied with their area are generally less fearful of crime.

Another important finding is that the urban/rural divide appears to be much more influential with respect to fear of crime than either religious composition or class divisions between the communities. These findings challenge the importance placed on religion in determining fear of crime. This is especially relevant in Northern Ireland where much emphasis is placed on religious divisions - even when accounting for fear of crime. For example, results from the Northern Ireland Crime Survey (Boyle and Haire, 1996) show that 37 per cent of Catholics, as opposed to 42 per cent of Protestants, were either 'very' or 'fairly' worried about becoming a victim of a terrorist attack, suggesting a higher proportion of Protestants feel unsafe in comparison to Catholics.

Table 4.1 Respondents' Fear of Crime - Day and Night-time

'Thinking about this area, how safe from ordinary crime do you feel walking alone around here during the day / night-time?'

	Catholic Lower Working Class Urban	Protestant Lower Working Class Urban	Mixed Middle Class Urban	Catholic Small Towns	Protestant Small Towns
Very Safe					
Day	62.3	76.6	61.2	91.6	88.8
Night-time	29.7	37.1	27.0	67.7	57.6
Safe					
Day	27.9	20.7	34.0	4.7	8.2
Night-time	42.6	30.9	45.9	20.7	23.3
A Bit Unsafe					
Day	5.7	0.5	2.2	0.0	0.9
Night-time	20.4	21.4	23.7	8.1	12.2
Very Unsafe					
Day	3.3	1.7	2.6	3.4	1.6
Night-time	6.2	6.9	2.4	2.8	3.4
Don't Know					
Day	0.8	0.5	0.0	0.3	0.4
Night-time	1.0	3.7	0.9	0.7	3.4

(Weighted Data)

Our results, however, show that those from both the segregated Catholic and Protestant lower working class communities are not that different to each other in terms of their fear of crime, despite their religious differences. Rather, the major differences that occur are between those living in the urban as opposed to the small town communities. Similarly, in relation to social class, the differences in relation to fear of crime are not so obvious between the upper middle class and lower working class communities as they are between the urban and rural or small town communities. Hence, it appears that the community in which one lives may be a better predictor of fear of crime than such factors as the religion of the respondent.

Worry about Specific Incidents

Apart from general fear of crime, the respondents were asked how worried they were about specific incidents occurring such as burglary, offences against the person, vehicle theft and sectarian attacks.

Table 4.2   Respondents' Worries about Burglary, Assaults and Threats

Burglary - 'How much do you worry about having your home broken into?'
Assaults - 'Sometimes people are assaulted or attacked - by fists, by kicks or by weapons - is this something you worry about?' (Excluding sexual attacks)
Threats - 'Sometimes people or their families are threatened with violence or with damage to their property - is this something you worry about?' (Excluding domestic violence and sectarian violence)

	Catholic Lower Working Class Urban	Protestant Lower Working Class Urban	Mixed Middle Class Urban	Catholic Small Towns	Protestant Small Towns
Very worried					
Burglary	10.9	11.4	8.2	3.8	5.8
Assaults	3.5	1.8	0.8	1.8	1.2
Threats	2.4	0.5	1.5	1.5	0.4
Fairly worried					
Burglary	37.2	23.4	31.1	23.4	19.2
Assaults	14.3	11.5	15.2	9.0	5.6
Threats	11.0	6.2	9.8	4.4	4.1
Not very worried					
Burglary	25.3	28.3	46.0	27.3	25.3
Assaults	39.4	17.9	44.1	16.8	9.0
Threats	37.3	13.4	35.4	11.2	6.0
Not at all worried					
Burglary	26.6	36.9	14.7	45.5	49.7
Assaults	42.8	68.7	39.9	72.4	84.3
Threats	49.3	79.9	53.2	82.9	89.4

(Unweighted Data)

In relation to burglary, the respondents were asked 'how much do you worry about having your home broken into?'. It is clear from the results that a relatively large proportion (between 48 to 25 per cent) of those interviewed from the different communities said they were either 'fairly worried' or 'very worried' about being burgled (Table 4.2). Those from the small town communities were the least concerned with only 25 to 27 per cent of those from the Catholic and Protestant small towns reporting that they were 'fairly' or 'very worried'. The respondents from the small towns were most likely to report that they were 'not at all' worried about being burgled. In contrast, those from the urban areas were more likely to say that they were worried about being burgled: 48 to 35 per cent said they were 'fairly' or 'very worried'.

Within the urban areas, however, the degree of worry was not evenly spread across the communities. For example, it was not found that those from the lower working class communities were consistently either more or less worried than those from the upper middle class areas. The only real exception to this was in relation to being 'not at all worried'. In this category, only 15 per cent of those from the middle class areas as opposed to 27 to 50 per cent of those from the lower working class areas said they were not at all worried about being burgled. Nonetheless, of all the specific offences, burglary caused the most concern for respondents.

The respondents were asked about their fears of personal assaults and threats. It is evident that fewer respondents were worried about personal offences than property offences like burglary (see above), with only 7 to 18 per cent saying they were 'very' or 'fairly worried' about being assaulted and 5 to 13 per cent were worried about being threatened (see Table 4.2). There were also a number of differences between the communities. Those from the mixed middle class urban and Catholic lower working class areas were less likely to say they were 'not at all worried' about personal offences than those from the other communities. For example only 39 and 43 per cent of those from the Catholic lower working class and mixed upper middle class said they were 'not at all worried' about being assaulted in comparison to 69 to 84 per cent of those in the other communities. Also, as with burglary, those from the small towns and Protestant lower working class were less worried about personal offences than those from the other communities. Indeed, the Protestant lower working class areas provide an obvious exception in that they consistently reported lower levels of worry than those in the other urban areas.

In relation to vehicle crime, it is apparent that those from the lower working class urban communities were clearly more worried about their vehicles being stolen or vandalised than respondents from other areas. Some 50 per cent and 32 per cent of those from the Catholic and Protestant lower working class communities respectively said they were 'very' or 'fairly worried' about their car being stolen in comparison to only between 7 to 23 per cent of those in the other communities. By contrast, those from the small town areas appeared to be the least concerned, with only 7 to 13 per cent saying they were worried about their car being stolen. It appears that the differing levels of worry clearly correspond to local concerns about car crime and joyriding, as reported earlier (see Table 2.5 - chapter two). These results showed higher levels of concern about car crime in the urban areas than the small town communities. However, although such worries were linked with local concerns, it appears that they also correspond closely to individuals witnessing such events and the differing levels of concern in the local communities (see Table 3.11 - chapter three).

Table 4.3   Respondents' Worries about Theft and Vandalism of a Vehicle

Theft - 'How much have you worried about the vehicle(s) being stolen?' (Only respondents with vehicles)
Vandalism - 'How much have you worried about the vehicle being vandalised?' (Only respondents with vehicles)

	Catholic Lower Working Class Urban	Protestant Lower Working Class Urban	Mixed Middle Class Urban	Catholic Small Towns	Protestant Small Towns
Very worried					
Theft	24.3	18.2	8.4	5.2	0.0
Vandalism	27.2	11.5	5.4	4.3	2.4
Fairly worried					
Theft	25.4	14.2	14.1	8.2	7.1
Vandalism	29.6	26.4	22.8	17.2	17.5
Not very worried					
Theft	26.6	25.7	43.0	27.0	14.2
Vandalism	20.1	23.6	43.5	18.0	12.8
Not at all worried					
Theft	23.1	41.9	34.5	59.7	78.7
Vandalism	23.1	38.5	28.4	60.5	67.3

(Unweighted Data)

A number of questions were asked in order to probe the issue of sectarian crime. These questions were designed to discover if the individual felt that a crime occurred directly because of sectarianism. Here for example, it was found that when respondents were asked if they worried about their home being damaged because of their religion, only a relatively small proportion admitted to being worried and only between 2 to 14 per cent said they were either 'very' or 'fairly worried'. Again, there were a number of significant differences between the community types, especially for those who said they were 'not at all worried'. For instance, those from the small town areas and Protestant lower working class communities were the least worried about such crime, with some 92 to 93 per cent saying they were 'not at all worried' (see Table 4.4 below). On the other hand, those from the Catholic lower working class and mixed middle class urban areas appeared to be more concerned about sectarian crime. Only between 53 and 56 per cent of those interviewed from these respective areas were 'not at all worried' about their home being damaged because of their religion.

The same general pattern is revealed in relation to worries about physical attacks of a sectarian nature (see Table 4.4 below) and differences are particularly noticeable between the Catholic and Protestant lower class communities. Many more of those from the Protestant lower class communities said they were 'not at all worried' (88 per cent) by comparison to those from the Catholic lower class communities (only 49 per cent). The reason for this difference is not clear, given that both communities are largely similar as they are urban, lower working class and segregated. One possible explanation may be that Catholic respondents are generally more worried than Protestant respondents. However, this was not found to be the case across the communities. For example, in the small town areas, a roughly similar low level of worry was expressed by those in both the Catholic and Protestant communities. Furthermore, in the mixed middle class communities where around half of the respondents were either Catholic or Protestant, it was found that a similar proportion of both Catholic and Protestant respondents expressed the same levels of worry. So, Catholics in the mixed middle class communities were not more worried than their Protestant counterparts. It is clear, therefore, that the differences in worry about sectarian offences are not simply driven by the religion of the respondent. Rather, it appears that such worries may be more directly related to the communities and environments in which people live.

Table 4.4   Respondents' Worries about Sectarian Crime - Home Damage, Physical Attack and Terrorist Attack

Home damage - 'How worried are you about your house being damaged because of your religion?'
Physical Attack - 'How worried are you about being subject to a physical attack because of your religion?'
Terrorist attack - 'How worried are you about being the victim of a bomb or other terrorist / paramilitary attack?'

	Catholic Lower Working Class Urban	Protestant Lower Working Class Urban	Mixed Middle Class Urban	Catholic Small Towns	Protestant Small Towns
Very worried					
Home damage	2.6	1.4	2.9	0.7	0.3
Physical attack	6.5	0.6	2.4	0.6	0.1
Terrorist attack	9.5	3.2	2.3	2.8	1.2
Fairly worried					
Home damage	11.2	2.4	4.3	2.1	2.1
Physical attack	11.2	6.2	4.5	3.6	0.6
Terrorist attack	22.4	16.9	9.5	7.6	10.6
Not very worried					
Home damage	33.0	2.8	36.7	4.9	4.8
Physical attack	33.3	5.7	39.8	6.9	4.8
Terrorist attack	24.2	26.7	42.1	10.1	11.3
Not at all worried					
Home damage	53.2	93.4	56.0	92.3	92.8
Physical attack	49.0	87.6	53.3	89.0	94.4
Terrorist attack	43.9	59.2	46.1	79.6	76.9

(Unweighted Data)

This is not to suggest that the higher level of fear found in the Catholic, rather than Protestant, lower working class communities is in some way irrational or unjustified. It may well be that such fears are rooted in the nature of the conflict in Northern Ireland. For example, it has been argued that much Catholic sectarian crime has been targeted at the police, army and state apparatus. On the other hand, much Protestant sectarian crime has been directed more randomly at Catholics, or Catholics associated with the Republican movement to those living in areas thought of as Republican (Bruce, 1992; Bowyer Bell, 1993; Coogan, 1995). Many of the Catholic lower working class communities chosen in this study would symbolise this. In effect, it could be argued that those living in the Catholic lower working class communities may have been more likely to think of themselves as 'potential targets' of sectarian crime and were therefore more likely to report it as a worry.

By contrast, concerns about being the victim of a bomb or other terrorist/paramilitary attack produced a different pattern of responses (see Table 4.4 below). A higher proportion of those from the lower working class communities said they were 'fairly worried' or 'very worried' than those from the other areas and this was especially the case for those from the Catholic lower working class communities. Worry about such incidents is clearly related to the type of community in which the respondent lives. The most dramatic differences found were those living in the small town areas, where between 77 per cent to 80 per cent of the respondents said they were 'not at all worried' about terrorist attacks as opposed to those in the urban areas, where the figures were only between 44 per cent to 59 per cent (see Table 4.4).

Perceptions of Crime in Northern Ireland and Elsewhere

In order to further explore the issue of fear of crime from a different perspective, the respondents were asked to compare their perceptions of the levels of 'ordinary' crime in their communities to other areas and to the rest of Northern Ireland. They were also asked if they thought the levels of crime had changed during the period of the cease-fires (as the interviews were held shortly after the end of the first set of paramilitary cease-fires in 1996 which had lasted sixteen months and ended with the London Docklands bombing).

Despite the very differing social and environmental conditions across the communities and the fact that some communities experienced high levels of social and economic deprivation, only a minority of respondents actually felt there was 'a lot more' or even 'a little more' crime in their area than the rest of Northern Ireland. In fact, only between 1 to 13 per cent of the respondents felt there was 'a lot more' or 'a little more' crime in their communities than the rest of Northern Ireland. Even for those in the segregated urban lower working class communities, only 13 to 8 per cent said they felt there was more crime in their areas (see Table 4.5). Such findings demonstrate that many people appear to see crime affecting other areas and not theirs. In a sense, it appears to be seen as someone else's problem or something that goes on in other areas. This was despite the fact that these communities were some of the most disadvantaged areas in Northern Ireland.

The most noticeable difference between the communities was with respect to respondents from the small town and urban areas. As expected, those in the small towns were most likely to say there was 'a lot less' crime in their communities than those from the urban communities. It is also evident that more of those from the Catholic and Protestant lower working class communities felt the crime levels in their areas were 'about the same' as the rest of Northern Ireland, while those from the middle class mixed areas were more likely to have said there was 'a little less' crime. So, while there were differences between the communities, especially regarding the extent to which they were seen as suffering from crime, the more general picture that emerged was that crime problems were things that occurred elsewhere or in other communities.

Comparing perceived levels of ordinary crime to Britain, it is evident that the majority of respondents from the communities felt that there was 'a little less' or 'a lot less' crime in Northern Ireland (Table 4.5 below). Indeed, only a minority of respondents felt that it was 'about the same' as Britain (between 9 to 16 per cent) and even fewer felt there was either 'a little more' or 'a lot more' crime (only between 3 to 7 per cent). In general, the respondents from the various communities felt Northern Ireland was a safer place and suffered from less crime than Britain.

The same question was asked in relation to the Republic of Ireland. Again it was found that the majority of respondents felt that there was less ordinary crime in Northern Ireland than in the Republic (see Table 4.5). However, more respondents claimed they did not know and this was especially the case for the Protestant lower working class and Protestant small town communities where 42 and 39 per cent respectively said they did not know how much crime there was in southern Ireland. Generally, however, it appears that respondents felt there was less crime in Northern Ireland than Britain or the Republic of Ireland, and that the difference was greatest between Northern Ireland and Britain. Britain was perceived to have the most crime.

Considering Northern Ireland's portrayal in the media as an essentially dangerous place, these findings may surprise some people. However, it is clear that people living in Northern Ireland are more aware of the risks and, conflict aside, they see Northern Ireland as a place less affected by the problems of crime than either Great Britain or the Republic of Ireland.

Table 4.5 Respondents' Perceptions of the Relative Extent of Ordinary Crime in the Communities in Comparison to the Rest of Northern Ireland, Great Britain and the Republic of Ireland

Rest of Northern Ireland. - 'Compared to the rest of Northern Ireland how much ordinary crime would you say there is in this area?'
To Great Britain - 'Compared to Britain how much ordinary crime would you say there is in Northern Ireland?'
To Eire - 'Compared to the Republic of Ireland, how much ordinary crime would you say there is in Northern Ireland?'

	Catholic Lower Working Class Urban	Protestant Lower Working Class Urban	Mixed Middle Class Urban	Catholic Small Towns	Protestant Small Towns
A lot more					
Rest of NI	3.3	1.2	0.2	0.1	0.3
To GB	1.4	1.0	0.0	1.0	0.0
To Eire	1.7	0.0	1.4	2.6	1.3
A little more					
Rest of NI	9.2	7.2	4.2	1.0	2.1
To GB	5.8	4.8	3.1	4.7	4.1
To Eire	5.1	6.9	7.7	8.4	17.2
About the same					
Rest of NI	40.8	49.3	26.9	22.5	9.77
To GB	9.2	16.6	12.0	10.2	10.3
To Eire	16.6	19.7	24.1	26.9	16.6
A little less					
Rest of NI	30.6	31.1	42.8	35.2	29.2
To GB	34.4	43.5	48.7	36.7	43.0
To Eire	48.9	23.9	35.1	25.7	17.3
A lot less					
Rest of NI	12.0	5.9	21.1	39.7	55.1
To GB	47.9	26.1	30.8	43.4	33.5
To Eire	18.8	7.7	11.9	16.0	7.8
DK/N.A.					
Rest of NI	4.1	5.4	4.7	1.5	3.7
To GB	1.3	8.0	5.4	4.0	9.1
To Eire	8.9	41.8	20.9	20.4	39.8

(Weighted Data)

Finally, the respondents were asked if they felt that the ordinary crime rate had changed in their area, and in Northern Ireland generally, during the period of the cease-fires. This was to assess whether during the period of cease-fires, when there was a relaxation of the security situation and arguably a lot less tension, there was a perception of less crime. It was found, however, that the majority of respondents reported that crime had either remained the same or had actually increased during the cease-fire (See Table 4.6). Indeed between 79 to 90 per cent of the respondents thought it had stayed the same or even increased, while only between 9 to 14 per cent felt crime had decreased either a little or a lot in their communities.

Table 4.6   Respondents' Perceptions of the Extent of Crime in the Communities and in Northern Ireland generally During the Period of the Cease-fires

Community - 'How much would you say the crime rate (ordinary) here (this area) changed during the cease-fires?'
Northern Ireland - 'In Northern Ireland would you say the crime rate (ordinary) changed during the period of the cease-fires?'

	Catholic Lower Working Class Urban	Protestant Lower Working Class Urban	Mixed Middle Class Urban	Catholic Small Towns	Protestant Small Towns
A lot more					
Community	6.5	2.8	1.5	0.7	0.6
N. Ireland	7.8	6.4	4.1	8.3	6.5
A little more					
Community	22.5	16.4	19.9	16.1	9.5
N. Ireland	25.9	21.6	46.3	22.6	24.1
About the same					
Community	51.0	59.5	60.5	67.6	80.0
N.Ireland	44.5	50.8	32.3	34.3	38.3
A little less					
Community	12.0	11.9	7.6	10.9	6.2
N.Ireland	12.6	12.9	7.8	20.4	19.8
A lot less					
Community	2.1	1.2	1.0	2.5	0.0
N.Ireland	1.0	1.5	0.7	4.1	1.5

(Weighted Data)

Similar to previous questions, it was found that when the question of crime was directed towards their community, rather than Northern Ireland as a whole, slightly fewer felt the crime rate had increased 'a little' or 'a lot' more. Nonetheless, what is clear from these findings is that people's perceptions of the extent of crime did not fall during the period of the cease-fires, in fact many felt it increased. This is despite a period when there had been a relaxation in the general security situation and arguably an increase in the 'feel good' factor.

Accounting for such findings is difficult in retrospect, but it could be linked to such factors like the reporting of crime in the media before and after the cease-fire. For instance, during the cease-fires, it could be argued media attention focused less on terrorist crime, which had obviously dramatically decreased, and more on everyday issues including ordinary crime. This may have led to the impression of more ordinary crime occurring during the cease-fires. However, that said, it is difficult to fully account for such changes in the perceptions of the respondents and this is only one possible explanation in accounting for the perceived upsurge in crime during the cease-fire.

Conclusions

The results from this chapter show how worries and fears of crime and victimisation are very much linked to the community in which people live. With regard to general worries, it was found that those living in small towns were much less concerned about crime than those in the urban areas. For example, between 89 to 92 per cent of those in small towns said they felt 'very safe' walking around their community in comparison to 77 to 62 per cent of those in urban areas. Respondents from small towns also reported lower levels of worry about specific criminal events. For instance, only between 4 to 6 per cent of those from small towns reported that they were very worried about having their home broken into as opposed to 8 to 11 per cent in the urban communities. Despite these differences, it was apparent from the results that most of the respondents felt safe in their area. Indeed, over 90 per cent reported feeling safe or very safe walking around their community during the day.

Similar to other surveys (e.g., Hough 1995; Mirrlees-Black and Allen, 1998), feelings of safety were also lower at night than during the day, and women were more likely to say they felt unsafe than men. Between 15 to 20 per cent of the women said they felt a bit or very unsafe at night in comparison to just 7 to 11 per cent of men. 72 to 88 per cent of respondents said they felt safe or very safe at night in comparison to over 90 per cent during the day. Nonetheless, despite the differences between day and night time and between men and women, it was clear that the same pattern of differences between the communities in terms of fear of crime was evident whereby those living in the small towns reported lower levels of worry than those in the urban communities.

Within the urban communities, the pattern of worry about crime was different than expected. It was found that those in the lower working class communities did not report significantly higher levels of worry than those in the upper middle class areas. This was despite the very different problems and social conditions reported in chapter two. It appears that worries expressed by the respondents in these communities more closely approximated general indicators of satisfaction with the areas than the differing problems and social conditions experienced within them (see chapter two).

It is clear from the results that there were differences in the amount of worry expressed about the differing types of incidents. Like many previous studies (e.g., Hough, 1995; Mirrlees-Black and Allen, 1998), it was found that the respondents were generally more worried about property-related crime than they were about personal crimes like assaults. So, while between 25 to 48 per cent of the respondents said they were either 'fairly worried' or 'very worried' about having their home broken into, only 7 to 18 per cent said they were 'fairly worried' or 'very worried' about being assaulted. Furthermore, although levels of worries about vehicle crime (including thefts and vandalism) were high in all communities, the respondents in the Catholic lower working class communities reported especially high levels of concern about this type of crime. This high level of concern in the Catholic lower working class communities also corresponded with the high proportion of individuals that had witnessed car crime and joyriding in these communities (as reported in chapter three).

With respect to sectarian crime, lower levels of worry were found in the small town communities than most of the urban communities. For example between 92 and 93 per cent of those from the small towns reported that they were not at all worried about having their homes damaged in a sectarian attack while only 53 to 56 per cent of those in the Catholic lower working class and mixed upper middle class urban communities said they were not at all worried about such incidents occurring. Surprisingly, those from the Protestant lower working class communities were less worried about sectarian crime (particularly physical attacks and having their home damaged) than those from any of the other urban communities. These results show how worries can be closely linked to particular types of communities and how levels of worry do not necessarily follow clear patterns like differences according to class or differences in urban and rural areas.

The results also demonstrate how people appear to view the problem of crime as something that affects other areas rather than their own communities. So even in the lower working class communities there was the perception that crime levels in their areas were about the same or actually lower than those found in the rest of Northern Ireland. The respondents also felt that there was more crime in other areas like Great Britain or the Republic of Ireland than in their own communities.

These results clearly show the importance of community related factors in accounting for differences in the fear of crime. What is also apparent is the *relative* importance of individually based factors like the sex, class or religion of respondents. While these were found to be important, they did not by any means fully account for the differences found in the worries and fears. To demonstrate this point, it is worth looking back to the question of how safe people felt walking around their community. If fear of crime was directly related to individual factors, such as religion, then similar levels of fear within groups of Catholics and Protestants would be expected. However, it is obvious that there were very different responses from those of the *same* religion living in differing communities. For example, 28 per cent of those in the Protestant lower working class as opposed to only 16 per cent in the Protestant small towns felt 'a bit unsafe' or 'very unsafe'. Similarly for factors like social class, if this was responsible for differing levels of worry than one would have expected the lower working class communities to have much higher levels of fear than the upper middle class communities. However, the results were very different, with more of those from the Protestant lower working class communities actually reporting that they felt very safe than those from the upper middle class communities.

These results therefore, unlike much of the previous research, demonstrate the importance of analysing issues such as the fear of crime with an appreciation of the powerful effect of community and community-based factors (O'Mahony D. and Quinn K. 1999). They also show how communities differ from each other on a number of dimensions and prove that, in order to make sense of the experiences of people who live within them, it is necessary to explore both their lived experiences in the communities, as well as the characteristics of the individuals.

5 Policing and the Communities

Introduction

As has been previously stated, one of the theoretical premises for the local community crime survey was that it provided an opportunity for a more complete understanding of the range of views amongst the different communities on criminological related matters. Much of the survey data on community attitudes towards policing in Northern Ireland has focused upon the relatively high levels of satisfaction with the RUC (PANI, 1996), with Catholic/Nationalists generally less supportive and less positive than there Protestant/Unionist counterparts. Indeed survey data in the mid to late 1990's has continued to emphasise the divergences between Catholics and Protestants (McGarry & O'Leary, 1999 for an overview).

Some scholars have questioned the usefulness of such a 'divided society' model of understanding policing in the North of Ireland (Brewer 1993). For example, Brewer has argued that sections of the Catholic community are not alienated from the RUC (Brewer, 1993). Similarly McVeigh (1994) has suggested that there are more tensions between working class Protestant youths and the RUC than is often assumed. We agree with such assertions. In our view, while the religion of respondents in survey data in Northern Ireland is a key feature, insufficient account has been taken of other variables such as age, sex, class or geographical area (Geary & Morison, 1992; O'Mahony & Quinn, 2000).

This chapter seeks to explore levels of satisfaction amongst the communities with regard to the police, how the respondents viewed their performance, whether they felt that the police treated people fairly and whether people actually would make use of the police service in response to a range of hypothetical events. It also examines whether respondents felt that people in their area made use of alternative sources of help and support in dealing with crime. While the latter category includes paramilitary groups (and produced some interesting findings in that area), it should be emphasised that this was only one of a range of responses from a spectrum of sources of assistance.

General Levels of Satisfaction with the Police

Previous research on levels of satisfaction with the policing service in Northern Ireland have been largely positive with some marked differences between Catholic and Protestant respondents and variances over time (Gallagher, 1995; Breen, 1995; PANI, 1996; PANI, 1998). For example, a recent survey carried out by the Police Authority found that 69 per cent of respondents considered the policing service to be 'very or fairly good', with 78 per cent of Protestants and 55 per cent of Catholics subscribing to this view (PANI 1998, p.10). There is some evidence to suggest that variances in Catholic attitudes in particular may vary in part dependent upon police conduct in high profile policing operations such as the policing of Drumcree and other public order events related to the marching season (Bryett, 1997). Such a variable is important with regard to the timing of the fieldwork for the Northern Ireland Communities Crime Survey. Fieldwork was carried out in the Spring of 1996, before the RUC 'U Turn' which forced the Orange march down the Garvaghy Rd. As has been acknowledged by the Chief Constable and the Police Authority, that decision had a clearly deleterious effect on RUC relations with the Catholic community (Belfast Telegraph, 24th July 1996).

The survey firstly explores general levels of satisfaction regarding the performance of the police service amongst the communities. This is then developed into a broader framework by including questions on other areas of public service (including the Housing Executive, Street Cleaning Department and others). Again the rationale is to locate the service provided by the police as part of a wider range of services which contribute to the quality of life and social fabric of individuals within their local communities.

Respondents were asked how satisfied they felt with the service delivered by a range of public agencies. As can be seen in Table 1, the RUC scored higher than either the Housing Executive or the Street Cleaning Department in satisfaction ratings in all the communities, except in the Catholic lower working class communities.

General levels of satisfaction with the RUC were highest among the Protestant working class communities with 86 per cent of respondents declaring themselves as 'satisfied' or 'very satisfied' with the service provided. In the mixed middle class communities, and the Catholic and Protestant small towns levels of satisfaction (either 'very' or 'satisfied') were also all above 80 per cent.

Table 5.1   Respondents' Levels of Satisfaction with the RUC, Housing Executive and Street Cleaning Department

'How satisfied are you, generally speaking, with the service provided around here by...'

	Catholic Lower Working Class Urban	Protestant Lower Working Class Urban	Mixed Middle Class Urban	Catholic Small Towns	Protestant Small Towns
Very Satisfied					
Housing Exec.	7.2	5.0	1.6	2.1	3.5
RUC	1.4	21.1	18.5	25.0	25.1
Street Clean	22.5	16.1	17.5	15.0	33.3
Satisfied					
Housing Exec.	29.2	22.7	5.2	20.7	22.2
RUC	55.8	65.1	64.2	59.2	55.2
Street Clean	44.8	57.2	59.2	47.6	42.0
Unsatisfied					
Housing Exec.	17.8	14.4	0.7	8.6	10.1
RUC	9.5	7.4	7.9	7.4	11.9
Street Clean	22.1	17.9	16.7	10.8	10.9
Very Unsatisfied					
Housing Exec.	13.3	8.7	0.5	15.0	8.5
RUC	10.2	3.0	1.1	2.8	4.6
Street Clean	8.8	7.9	4.5	20.8	8.1
DK/NA					
Housing Exec.	32.4	49.2	92.1	53.7	55.7
RUC	23.1	3.5	8.2	5.7	3.2
Street Clean	1.8	1.0	2.1	5.8	5.7

(Weighted Data)

However, in the lower working class Catholic Communities, while 56 per cent of respondents declared themselves 'satisfied' with the service of the RUC, a sizeable minority of almost 20 per cent of respondents described themselves as either 'unsatisfied' or 'very unsatisfied' with the service. The next highest levels of dissatisfaction expressed were in the small Protestant towns where some 16 per cent expressed themselves as 'unsatisfied' or 'very unsatisfied'.

What was also of interest in relation to the question concerning RUC service was the high numbers of 'Do not Know/Not Applicable' in the lower working class Catholic communities - some 23 per cent of respondents. This compared to only 3 per cent of respondents in the Protestant small towns and 4 to 8 percent of those in the other communities. If one looks at other Do not Know/Not Applicable answers to other questions, (such as the figure of 92 per cent with regard to the Housing Executive question posed to mixed middle class areas where few residents lived in Housing Executive owned premises) and the significantly lower numbers of do not know/not applicable responses to this policing question amongst the other communities, then an interesting picture appears to emerge.

Substantial number of respondents in the lower working class Catholic communities either held no view or felt that the question of the police delivering a service to them was not applicable. While it is impossible to speculate with any degree of certainty as to the reasons for such a high Don't/Know response rate, the comparison with Housing Executive question in the mixed middle class areas is interesting. Respondents in middle class areas did not live in Housing Executive houses, the Housing Executive did not deliver a service to them, they had no experience of such a service and therefore the question was not relevant. The perceived lack of a police service delivered to a considerable number of respondents from lower working class Catholic areas, discussed in further detail below, may have led respondents to consider the notion of a police service being delivered to them as irrelevant.

Reporting Crime to the Police

Levels of reporting of crime to the police in Northern Ireland have been previously found to be comparatively low in some studies. For example, the International Crime Victims Survey found that Northern Ireland had the lowest levels of reporting offences to the police (47 per cent, compared to an average of 50 per cent with the most common reason given that it was 'not serious enough' or there was 'no loss' (51 per cent), although 6 per cent also gave as their reason fear or dislike of the police (Mayhew and van Dijk, 1997). A similar picture emerged in the Northern Ireland Community Crime Survey with, once again, significant variations between the communities.

In terms of burglaries, for example, only 68 per cent of respondents who had been burgled in Catholic lower working class urban communities had reported it to the police, compared to 93 per cent of those in Protestant lower working class urban communities, 97 per cent in mixed middle class urban communities and in Catholic and Protestant small towns 88 per cent and 94 per cent respectively. When asked their reason for not reporting victimisation 8 per cent of respondents in Catholic lower working class urban communities said it was fear or dislike of the police, a response that was non-existent or minimal in the other communities.

Table 5.2   Percentage of Respondents stating that they would 'Very Likely' Report the Incident to the Police

	Catholic Lower Working Class Urban	Protestant Lower Working Class Urban	Mixed Middle Class Urban	Catholic Small Towns	Protestant Small Towns
Home broken into	85.0	98.0	99.0	97.0	99.0
Damage to outside of house	54.0	81.0	87.0	83.0	88.0
Theft of something you are carrying	59.0	87.0	89.0	80.0	86.0
Assault with fists, kicks or weapons	56.0	82.0	87.0	79.0	87.0
Threat to hurt or damage	43.0	76.0	72.0	62.0	71.0

(Weighted Data)

Given the relatively low number of victims encountered in most victimisation surveys, it was decided that a series of hypothetical scenarios should be offered to *all* respondents in order to elicit their likelihood of reporting a crime to the police if they were themselves a victim of a crime or if they witnessed a crime occurring. With the first set of scenarios respondents were asked about their likelihood of reporting any of a number of incidents to the police.

In every hypothetical victimisation scenario, respondents from the working class Catholic areas were the least likely to respond by calling the police. Similarly when respondents were asked how they would respond to less immediate forms of victimisation (such as witnessing vandalism or young people making noise outside the home), once again respondents from working class Catholic communities were the least likely to respond by calling the police. For example, 7 per cent of respondents from the working class Catholic areas, compared to 36 per cent from the working class Protestant areas, 42 per cent from the mixed middle class areas, 29 per cent from the Catholic small towns and 45 per cent from the Protestant small towns indicated that they would respond to noise outside their home by calling the police. Similarly with regard to witnessing a crime such as vandalism, only 21 per cent of respondents from the working class Catholic areas, compared to 45 per cent from the Protestant working class areas, 72 per cent from the mixed middle class areas, 59 per cent from the Catholic small towns and 67 per cent from the Protestant small towns indicated that they would call the police.

Personal Knowledge of Police Officers

Respondents in the NICCS were also asked if they knew a police officer either by sight or to speak to. Respondents from the Protestant small towns were most likely to know a police officer 'by sight' (76 per cent) and they were also most likely to know a police officer 'to speak to' (49 per cent).

The next highest figures were for the Catholic small towns where 43 per cent of respondents knew a police officer 'by sight' or 'to speak to'. 33 per cent of those from the mixed middle class and 34 per cent from the Protestant lower working class knew a police officer either 'by sight' or 'to speak to'. However in the Catholic lower class areas, 90 per cent of respondents did *not* know a police officer 'by sight' or 'to speak to' and in fact only 1 per cent of respondents actually knew a police officer 'to speak to'.

Table 5.3 Respondents' Personal Knowledge of the Police

'Do you know any Police Officers in this area to…'

	Catholic Lower Working Class Urban	Protestant Lower Working Class Urban	Mixed Middle Class Urban	Catholic Small Towns	Protestant Small Towns
To speak to	1.3	14.9	21.9	22.3	48.6
By sight	9.1	20.1	10.7	21.0	27.0
No, neither	87.7	65.1	67.3	56.3	24.2
DK	2.0	0.0	0.1	0.4	0.0

(Weighted Data)

Fairness of the Police

When respondents were asked how fairly they thought the police treated people in their areas a similar picture emerged. 73 per cent of respondents in the lower working class Protestant communities, 74 per cent in the Protestant small towns, 70 per cent in the Catholic small towns and 62 per cent in the mixed middle class areas felt that people in their area were treated 'fairly' or 'very fairly'. However only 36 per cent of respondents in the lower working class Catholic areas felt similarly. Indeed 16 per cent of respondents in the Catholic lower working class areas felt that people in their area were treated 'unfairly' or 'very unfairly', compared to 5.5 per cent in the Protestant lower class areas, 2.5 per cent in the mixed middle-class areas, 4 per cent in the Catholic small towns and 4.3 per cent in the Protestant small towns.

More generally, respondents were asked if they thought that the police treated Catholics or Protestants throughout Northern Ireland better or if they were treated equally (see Table 6). Respondents from the Protestant lower working class areas (73 per cent) were most likely to think that the police treated Catholics and Protestants equally, followed by the Protestant small towns (69 per cent), mixed middle class (62 per cent) and Catholic small towns (50.5 per cent). In contrast, only 19 per cent of respondents in the working class Catholic areas felt that both Protestants and Catholics were treated equally.

Table 5.4   Respondents' Views Regarding Police Fairness in the Treatment of People in Northern Ireland as a Whole

	Catholic Lower Working Class Urban	Protestant Lower Working Class Urban	Mixed Middle Class Urban	Catholic Small Towns	Protestant Small Towns
Catholics treated better	0.7	8.7	2.0	0.3	3.5
Both treated equally	19.0	72.6	62.4	50.5	68.7
Protestants treated better	62.0	6.0	19.5	28.6	8.1
DK/refusal	18.3	12.7	16.2	20.7	19.7

(Weighted Data)

The Importance of Police Tasks

In order to further explore the distinctions in views between the communities, we looked in more detail at what the communities expected from their police service and their views as to how well these duties were performed. Respondents were asked to consider a range of normal police duties, which were subsequently grouped into three main categories for the purposes of analysis. These included (i) investigating and responding to crime including; 'ordinary' crime, terrorist crime, drug crime and responding to emergency calls (ii) crime prevention including; patrolling in cars and checking shop security, and (iii) community liaison including; visiting community projects, schools and youth clubs and providing crime prevention advice.

There was a degree of consensus amongst the communities with regard to the main duties of the police (see Table 6). Across all communities, 'responding to and investigating crimes' were ranked as the most important duties, particularly dealing with emergency calls and drug related problems. However, when the responses between the communities were examined more closely, marked differences were evident. The most obvious difference in response to these questions was that a significantly smaller proportion of the respondents from the lower working class

82 *Crime, Community and Locale*

Catholic communities ranked policing tasks as 'very important'. This appeared to be particularly the case when it entailed the police maintaining a presence in the area by walking the beat, visiting schools or community projects.

Table 5.5 Respondents' Views Regarding the Importance of Police Tasks (viewed as very important)

	Catholic Lower Working Class Urban	Protestant Lower Working Class Urban	Mixed Middle Class Urban	Catholic Small Towns	Protestant Small Towns
Respond to emergency calls	83.4	99.3	98.3	97	98.8
Investigating terrorist crime	70.0	93.5	95.2	90.8	95.4
Investigating ordinary crime	65.0	93.1	87.8	81.7	92.2
Dealing with drugs	80.0	99.2	91.4	98.1	98.5
Patrolling in cars	41.5	88.8	60.9	57.5	76.4
Walking the beat	39.1	87.5	72.4	62.8	75.9
Providing crime prevention advice	46.9	70.4	53.5	54.9	71.8
Visiting schools, and youth clubs	37.7	82.6	70.5	60.8	80.8

(Weighted Data) Table represents the aggregation of a number of responses

For example 41.5 per cent of those from the lower working class Catholic area felt that it was 'very important' for police to patrol in cars, as compared to 89 per cent of those from the equivalent Protestant areas. The equivalent figures for the middle class area was 61 per cent, 57 per cent for the Catholic small towns and 76 per cent for the Protestant towns. In terms of walking the beat, 39 per cent of respondents from the lower working class Catholic communities felt that this was 'very important', compared to 87.5 per cent from the lower working class Protestant areas, 72 per cent of mixed middle class respondents, 62 per cent of Catholic small town and 76 per cent of Protestant small town dwellers who felt that it was 'very important'. Again in terms of visiting schools, 38 per cent of respondents from lower working class areas versus 83 per cent of those from lower working class Protestant areas, 70 per cent of mixed middle class, 61 per cent of Catholic small town and 81 per cent of Protestant small town respondents viewed it as 'very important'.

Whilst views as to the importance of an issue such as 'dealing with drugs' were generally more uniform, significant differences again appeared amongst the respondents from the Catholic lower working class areas. 80 per cent of respondents in those areas viewed it as 'very important' compared to 99 per cent in the lower class Protestant areas, 91 per cent in the mixed middle class, 98 per cent in the Catholic and Protestant small towns. Even with regard to 'responding to emergency calls', where the responses are between 97 per cent and 99 per cent for all other communities, a comparatively low 83 per cent of respondents from the lower working class Catholic areas viewed this duty as 'very important'. It would appear therefore that there are clear differences in what different communities expect from the police, particularly in the lower working class Catholic areas. Further, it would appear that expectations are also influenced by whether or not police activities would require a police presence in the area.

Crime Management and 'Other' Organisations

The NICCS also sought to explore whether other organisations in the community dealt with crime related matters. While there is a substantial literature on the involvement of Republican and Loyalist paramilitaries in 'policing' activities in Northern Ireland (e.g. Morrissey & Pease, 1982; Munck, 1988; Hillyard, 1985; Bell, 1996; Conway, 1997), this survey sought data on whether other groups such as community organisations, residents associations, church groupings etc were also involved in dealing with crime and its consequences, what Brewer et al (1997. p. 165) refer to as 'local crime management'.

This element of the survey was approached on three levels:
(i) all respondents were asked a simple yes/no as to whether any other groups were engaged in dealing with crime in their area,
(ii) all respondents were asked which types of groups were engaged in these activities and
(iii) those who had replied yes to the question were asked whether the groups mentioned were engaged specifically in dealing with a broad

spectrum of 'policing' type duties. i.e. (a) dealing with nuisance, (b) dealing with property crimes and (c) dealing with crimes of violence.

Once again there are very clear distinctions across the range of communities. In response to the first question, 41 per cent of respondents from the lower working class Catholic areas, 27 per cent from the lower working class Protestant areas, 5 per cent from the mixed middle class areas, 2 per cent from the small Catholic towns and 3 per cent from the small Protestant town indicated that other organisations were involved in dealing with crime in their area. Of those who indicated 'yes', the vast majority of respondents referred to either Republican or Loyalist paramilitaries dealing with crime (see Table 8). As one would expect, paramilitary activity was seen as much more common in relation to dealing with crime in the lower working class Catholic and Protestant communities, but it was also marginally higher in middle class areas in greater Belfast than in the small Catholic and Protestant towns outside Belfast.

Table 5.6   Respondents' Reporting to Other Organisations Dealing with Crime in Their Area

	Catholic Lower Working Class Urban	Protestant Lower Working Class Urban	Mixed Middle Class Urban	Catholic Small Towns	Protestant Small Towns
Community groups	2.7	0.7	0.2	0.0	0.3
Residents associations	0.8	0.0	0.2	0.0	0.3
Republican / loyalist paramilitaries	35.8	25.8	4.3	1.8	2.5
Others	1.4	0.7	0.1	0.0	0.0
Total	40.7	27.2	4.8	1.8	2.1

(Weighted Data)

The response rates for other organisations dealing with crime such as Residents Associations and Community Groups were, as can be seen above, generally very low (see Table 5.6). The most active group, other than paramilitaries, were Community Groups in the lower working class Catholic communities, but even there only 3 per cent of respondents replied that these were active in dealing with crime. Active groups in the other communities were either very few or non-existent.

Those respondents who had said that there were other organisations engaged in dealing with crime in their area, were asked to consider a range of activities and to indicate whether the various organisations were involved in dealing with them. The issues were chosen to represent a spectrum of anti-social/criminal behaviour. The issues chosen were (i) Nuisance (ii) Property Crime, and (iii) Violent Crime. It is important to remember that only those who had answered yes to the question of whether other organisations were involved in dealing with crime were asked these specific questions.

The patterns with regard to the spectrum of offences shows interesting similarities to other findings in the survey. The largest numbers of respondents who said that Community Groups were involved in dealing with crime were found in the lower working class Catholic communities (see Table 5.7 below). Responses from the lower working class Catholic communities were broadly in line with the comparatively large numbers (36 per cent) of the total sample who had answered that paramilitaries were involved in dealing with crime. 71 per cent of the subsample of the Catholic lower working class respondents who answered 'yes' that other organisations were dealing with crime, replied that paramilitaries were engaged with dealing with nuisances. Similar figures of 65.5 per cent and 65 per cent of the subsample were recorded with regard to dealing with property crime and crimes of violence. Consistent with other findings with regard to attitudes to and use of the police in this survey, it would appear that a range of anti-social crime is perceived as being 'dealt with' by the paramilitaries in working class Catholic communities.

What was of equal interest, however, and the reason for providing a breakdown of the percentage of the subsamples who had answered 'yes', was that the figures in the working class Protestant areas did not correspond in the same manner. 26 per cent of the total sample in the lower working class Protestant areas replied that paramilitaries were involved in dealing with crime in their area. However when provided with the three anti-social/criminal offences of nuisance, property and violent crime, figures matching the activities of paramilitaries in dealing with these offences were quite low. Only 29 per cent of the subsample in the Protestant lower working class areas indicated that paramilitaries were dealing with nuisance in their area. The responses for crimes against property and crimes of violence were even lower with 20 per cent and 14 per cent respectively of the sub-sample replying that these were issues being dealt with by paramilitaries.

Table 5.7   Respondents Reporting that Other Organisations were Involved in Dealing with Certain Crime Related Issues

(% should be read in conjunction with the weighted numbers of actual respondents at the bottom of the columns in order not to give misleading impressions, particularly where the numbers of respondents are quite low).

	Catholic Lower Working Class Urban	Protestant Lower Working Class Urban	Mixed Middle Class Urban	Catholic Small Towns	Protestant Small Towns
Community groups					
Nuisance	11.8	2.4	2.0	15.4	0.0
Property crime	3.8	0.0	0.0	0.0	0.0
Violent crime	0.7	0.0	0.0	0.0	0.0
Residents associations					
Nuisance	1.4	0.0	7.8	23.1	0.0
Property crime	0.0	0.0	2.0	0.0	0.0
Violent crime	0.0	0.0	0.0	0.0	0.0
Paramilitaries					
Nuisance	71.4	29.6	15.7	15.4	10.5
Property crime	65.5	14.8	3.9	15.4	10.5
Violent crime	65.2	20.1	19.6	15.4	21.1
Other					
Nuisance	1.4	0.0	0.0	0.0	0.0
Property crime	1.4	0.0	0.0	0.0	0.0
Violent crime	4.2	0.0	0.0	0.0	0.0
Total Number	287	169	51	13	19

(Weighted Data)

In other words, while one quarter of the sample of respondents in lower working class Protestant areas indicated that paramilitaries were engaged in dealing with crime, the majority of those did not appear willing or able to match these activities with specific crimes.

Obviously a number of explanations might account for this apparent disparity. First, it may be that the range of offences chosen was insufficiently broad to pick up the activities in which Loyalist paramilitaries were engaged in 'dealing with'. Second, it may be that working class Protestant respondents are less knowledgeable about, or less willing to discuss the specific nature of the Loyalist paramilitaries' activities in 'dealing with' crime. Third, as some commentators have argued (Conway, 1997; Winston, 1997; McEvoy & Mika, 1998), unlike Republican paramilitaries, much Loyalist 'policing' activity is concerned with the internal policing of their own organisations and internecine disputes between factions rather than dealing with the range of anti-social behaviour and crime represented by nuisance, property or violent crime.

Conclusions

The methodology and findings of the Community Crime Survey have important implications for the future in terms of policing and criminal justice policy. As noted earlier, the findings do not represent a generalised, consensual view that can be 'averaged up' to apply to some idea of a homogeneous, 'everyperson' citizen of Northern Ireland but they do usefully reflect the reality that experiences and attitudes to policing vary considerably in different communities across Northern Ireland. For example we have shown that the experiences and attitudes of middle class Protestants and Catholics are often fundamentally different from that of lower working class Protestants and Catholics. Yet in much of the previous research and literature they are subsumed under their respective religious classifications, ignoring other relevant factors such as class, urban/rural divisions or community based differences. It was in order to address these issues that the NICCS selected specific communities on the basis of social deprivation, religious composition and urban/rural divides to ascertain differing (and similar) experiences and attitudes of respondents to crime and policing within these communities.

The difficulties of the relationship between the working class Catholic communities and the RUC was clearly underlined. Respondents from the working class Catholic communities were least satisfied with the RUC, had little personal knowledge of the RUC, were less likely to report crimes, were more likely to think that Catholics were treated unfairly and less likely to prioritise police functions which required a police presence in their communities. The problems of that interaction were further highlighted by a considerable acknowledgement (36 per cent) amongst respondents from working class Catholic areas of the involvement of paramilitaries in dealing with crime in their areas and a greater ability to match the activities of paramilitaries to dealing with specific crimes such as violence, property offences, or even nuisance.

The experiences and attitudes of the working class Protestant communities were also of considerable interest. For example, while some previous qualitative research has suggested a critical attitude towards the RUC from elements of the Protestant working class (e.g. McVeigh, 1994; Hamilton, Moore & Trimble, 1995; Brewer, Lockhart & Rodgers, 1997), this was by and large not reflected in our findings.

Respondents from working class urban Protestant communities had less personal knowledge of police officers than for example those from the Protestant small towns, with only 15 per cent knowing an officer to speak to compared to 49 per cent in the small Protestant towns. Nonetheless the highest satisfaction ratings, most positive views (from a police perspective) regarding the fair treatment of the public and specific evaluations of performance in areas such as investigating terrorist or ordinary crime, emergency responses or visiting schools and youth clubs were all recorded in the working class Protestant communities. Whether this is due to a 'loyalty' factor (see Patten, 1999) amongst working class Protestant respondents towards the police being more manifest when using quantitative survey techniques in particular rather than qualitative interviews is difficult to assess with any degree of certainty[1].

Finally with regard to the Protestant & Catholic small towns, perhaps of most interest were the similarities between respondents from these areas in terms of their views and experiences of crime and policing. For example there was considerable homogeneity between the Catholic and Protestant small town respondents regarding satisfaction with the RUC, fair treatment in the area and police performance. Interestingly however, there was some

---

[1] This was suggested by a number of the field-workers on the NICCS who juxtaposed some respondents' critical conversational comments regarding the RUC compared to more positive assessments when actually completing the survey. Such a thesis might be usefully explored using both qualitative and quantitative techniques and comparing the results.

disparity between the small towns regarding the police performance at dealing with drugs (30 per cent of Protestant small town dwellers responding that the police were doing a 'good' job compared to 17 per cent of Catholic respondents). When this was examined more closely, however, it was discovered that one small Catholic town in particular was particularly concerned about drugs, underlining again the significance of local variables in assessing views on crime and policing.

In the same way as the work of Kinsey 1984, Jones *et al.*, 1986, Crawford *et al.*, 1990 and others sought to critique of the official statistics as well as some of the cruder (at least) 'national' victimisation surveys, the NICCS has sought to explore some of the taken for granted realities about policing in this jurisdiction. The generally high levels of satisfaction and faith in the RUC of broader Northern Ireland surveys are not reflected evenly in the communities sampled in this study. While religion/political opinion is one variable in understanding those divisions, we accept the critique of a 'divided society' analysis offered by Brewer (1993; 1994) wherein views on policing do not divide neatly along sectarian lines.

However, in acknowledging the diversity of opinions amongst the communities in Northern Ireland regarding policing (eg in terms of the diversity between middle class and working class catholic communities), we are not suggesting that this should be interpreted as a 'watering down' of the case for structural change and reform of the RUC. Such a view would be analogous to suggesting that a police service in Britain should take comfort from the fact that any race relations problems are experienced most acutely by urban black working class communities.

The significance of localised crime surveys is that they represent a critical/empirical tool to represent a more detailed account of local communities, underlining a more holistic analysis. The characteristics of communities are investigated, rather than seeking to impose a particular ideal conception of how that community should appear (MacLean 1996:90). This survey, therefore, seeks to better articulate the particular location and nature of the problem of policing in Northern Ireland and sets up a bench-mark by which reform may be judged. Hence, it offers those currently tasked with changing Northern Ireland's policing service, in the wake of the Patten Report, with a clearer agenda as to the kind of change that is required if a Northern Ireland policing service is to command more widespread support and acceptance.

6 Securing the Home

Introduction

The most recent Royal Ulster Constabulary's (RUC) 'Report of the Chief Constable' (1999) contains the warning that Northern Ireland has undergone a significant increase in the amount of reported crime over the previous year. While other factors, such as victims willingness to report crimes, may partially account for this increase, it appears likely that there has been an actual increase in the levels of ordinary crime (RUC, 1999, p.12). This warning has been reiterated by the Patten Report, who go on to say that, 'A more normal security environment might therefore lead to more "normal" criminality.' (Patten, 1999, 13.6). Ordinary crime, as opposed to paramilitary offences, has for the first time become a dominant concern of policing and crime control discourse in Northern Ireland. Concurrent with this has been an increased emphasis and concern about crime prevention and measures to secure the home, which contrasts with the previous importance attached to such measures. For whilst crime prevention, together with other concerns of normal policing, has in the past been relevant in Northern Ireland, its message has been largely muted by concerns over the continuation of the conflict (Mulcahy, 1999).

The message constantly reiterated from the 1980s was that Northern Ireland was basically law abiding and relatively free from the problems of crime that plagued other communities. This message was channelled through the Reports of the Chief Constable, through international victimisation studies (e.g. Mayhew and van Dijk, 1997), and via fictional representations of crime in Northern Ireland (see, Kippax, 1993 p. 33; Petit, 1996 p. 399). Even if the situation was never quite as one journal depicted: '...you really can go out of your house and not bother to lock the front door' (Crane, 1982), the reality of risk was never fully considered. The image that was constantly emphasised was that, unless the individual was at risk from the conflict or sectarian violence, their home was relatively safe from the ravages of ordinary crime; crime prevention was a useful but not an urgent matter. It was irrelevant whether there was substance to that claim, since the absence of local victimisation studies (the inclusion of Northern Ireland in national and international victimisation studies has been a relatively recent development) means that there has been nothing to counter the prevailing view on ordinary crime and crime prevention.

The purpose of this chapter is to examine the measures that respondents in the different communities adopted to secure their homes and mitigate against the effects of crime, as well as the best means that they considered would prevent crime, and to consider those measures in the context of the new emphasis in the Chief Constable's Report on crime prevention. It will be argued that securing the home has had ramifications, not only for the households in the different communities in the past, but also for why there is a new emphasis on such security. That emphasis can be accounted for by a number of factors, including the increased amount of police time that can be devoted to ordinary crime, and the need for the RUC to be seen to be developing new roles in the light of anticipations about the Patten Report (Mulcahy, 1999), but also because of wider developments in how crime is perceived and how it should be managed. In this last context the question of home security has achieved a greater prominence through its relevance to the governmentality literature. O'Malley in particular has stressed the benefits to be accrued from this approach in relation to looking at crime prevention and insurance. He has argued that there has been a shift in the responsibility for crime prevention away from the state and towards the individual householder (O'Malley 1991; 1992; 1996). Agencies, governmental and non-governmental, now provide an expertise to allow the householder to come to an informed decision on the best means of providing for their own security and to take steps to mitigate against any loss through insurance. The householder is encouraged to perceive this as being in their own best interests and the police are not seen as bastions against crime but rather as facilators and partners in crime prevention. In this rationality '[T]he prudent subject of risk must be responsive, knowledgeable and rational. To rely on the state to deal with the harmful effects of known, calculable and individually manageable risks appears feckless and calculable' (O'Malley, 1996, p.202).

Crime Prevention

In this section respondents were asked about the steps they had taken to secure their homes; what influenced them to take those steps, their use of friends and neighbours to help secure their property if they were away from home, and whether they were insured against theft from their home. Respondents were also asked about what they considered to be the best crime prevention measures that could be adopted in their communities.

Firstly, respondents were asked whether their homes had had any security measures installed, or other precautions taken against intrusion, and whether they themselves had installed them. As can be seen in Table 6.1, there was a significant variation between the urban and small town communities. Properties in all of the urban communities had significantly higher levels extra security, particularly in the form of stronger doors and improved locks, which reflects the urban/small towns division in terms of feelings of safety.

Table 6.1   Security Measures in the Home

'Has your home been security upgraded with ...?' (% of respondents replying 'yes')

	Catholic Lower Working Class Urban	Protestant Lower Working Class Urban	Mixed Middle Class Urban	Catholic Small Towns	Protestant Small Towns
Stronger doors	34.9	20.0	40.6	16.1	15.8
Improved locks on doors and windows	45.5	42.4	67.6	24.8	25.0
Security chain on door	25.0	25.5	27.9	10.1	9.6
Burglar alarm	2.6	1.4	16.8	3.8	2.7
Security lighting on outside of house or block	21.5	7.9	34.7	15.0	18.8
Erection of fences or entrance gates around ground floor entrance	25.3	9.3	9.5	6.6	1.7
Spyhole in door	3.2	3.4	4.3	0.0	3.1

(Unweighted Data)

In terms of the urban communities, there were also significant variations in the numbers reporting having extra security measures. Respondents in mixed middle class communities were the most likely to have security measures, which may be a reflection of greater anxieties, insurance considerations, more affluence or a combination of these factors. As regards levels of safety, respondents in mixed middle class communities had not expressed greater levels of anxiety about being alone at night or worrying about the possibility of being burgled (see chapter four). When asked whether they worried about their home being broken into, 39 per cent of respondents from mixed middle class communities had expressed such a worry; either 'very worried' or 'fairly worried', compared to 48 per cent of respondents in Catholic lower working class urban communities and 35 per cent in Protestant lower working class urban communities. The extra security measures may, however, have assuaged middle class anxieties. In response to being asked what worry had prompted them to install a security measure, however, there was a significantly higher incidence of respondents in mixed middle class communities reporting that they had done so because of personal experience of crime (see Table 6.2). Though this may appear odd given the relatively low levels of victimisation found across the communities (see chapter three) in the previous twelve months, it could possibly be related to differences in victimisation over a much longer period.

There were also significant variations between Catholic and Protestant lower working class urban communities in terms of the nature of the security measures. Respondents in Protestant lower working class urban communities were less likely to have installed stronger doors, to have security lighting or to have fences around their properties. This may reflect differences in the types of intrusion that may be feared, for example a sectarian attack rather than a burglary, but also differences in housing structure and tenure.

Respondents in our survey also appeared to have taken fewer precautions than those included in surveys in Britain. For example, the 1998 British Crime Survey (BCS) found that 24 per cent of respondents had had a burglar alarm installed, 72 per cent had double locks or deadlocks on the outside of doors of their house and 71 per cent had window locks, (BCS, 1998, p.49). Similarly, the 1996 Scottish Crime Survey had corresponding figures of 16, 62 and 48 per cent (Scottish Office, 1998, p.64). Equally, the 1996 International Crime Victims Survey found that 27 per cent of respondents in England and Wales had a burglar alarm, as opposed to 25 per cent in Scotland and only 11 per cent in Northern Ireland. In terms of special door locks, the figures were 68 per cent in England and Wales, 63 per cent in Scotland and 35 per cent in Northern Ireland (Mayhew and van Dijk, 1997, Appendix 4, Table 18). Making direct comparisons between the different surveys can be problematic, but it does appear that, generally, people in our Northern Ireland communities sample have lower levels of security measures installed in their homes. It could be argued that if there is a continuing increase in the level of ordinary crime, a change in policing and the same rationality that applies in Britain is applied to Northern Ireland then these figures would be expected to increase significantly in the future.

Table 6.2   Installing Home Security

'If you did one of the above because you were worried about crime, was that worry based on ...?' (% of respondents replying 'yes')

	Catholic Lower Working Class Urban	Protestant Lower Working Class Urban	Mixed Middle Class Urban	Catholic Small Towns	Protestant Small Towns
Personal experience of crime	43.2	25.5	47.4	16.1	13.7
Police advice	7.6	5.6	1.4	4.6	5.9
Friends or neighbours	19.5	23.6	9.5	6.9	5.9
Advertising	8.1	11.8	2.9	4.6	3.9
Community group or voluntary organisation advice	2.7	0.6	0.3	0.0	2.0
TV programme, eg Crimewatch	23.8	1.2	1.1	4.6	6.9
Other	25.4	28.0	30.7	51.7	62.7
DK	5.4	10.6	7.5	16.1	5.9

(Unweighted Data)

Those respondents who had installed security measures were asked whether they had installed them themselves. A large majority had done so for each of the categories of security measures and in each of the communities. In terms of stronger doors and improved locks the lowest response for having installed them was still over 80 per cent, in the case of stronger doors in Catholic small town communities. Respondents who had taken security measures were then asked what had prompted them to do so.

As can be seen from Table 6.2, with the exception of the 'other' category the single largest factor for installing security devices in the home was a personal experience of crime and this was particularly so in urban communities. Those living in small towns had more multifarious reasons for installing security measures, and had a significantly lower response to the question as to whether their worry was based on personal experience of crime. This last point is different to the findings contained in chapter three, which suggested a much smaller variation of victimisation between urban and small town communities. This may be accounted for by the different time spans involved; the findings in chapter three were concerned with respondents who had been the victims of a crime within the past twelve months, while here the question is concerned with a possibly longer time period and the reason for security measures having been installed.

There were also significant variations between the urban communities. Those living in mixed middle class and Catholic lower working class urban communities had a significantly higher incidence of respondents stating that the reason for their having installed security measures was personal experience of crime, compared to those living in Protestant lower working class urban communities. Respondents in Catholic and Protestant lower working class urban communities were also more reliant on friends/neighbours and advertising for advice on security measures. It is also notable that a quarter of the respondents in Catholic lower working class urban communities stated that their worry was prompted by a TV programme, with the example being quoted to them of 'Crimewatch'. In chapter four the findings suggested that in Catholic lower working class urban communities there were higher levels of worry being expressed about crime, and it may be that such programmes reinforce or exacerbate such worries rather than create them (Sparks,1992).

Empty Properties

Respondents were asked whether they informed anyone if they left their property empty for any considerable period. Respondents in Catholic lower working class urban communities were more likely to inform neighbours, relatives and/or friends that their house was empty compared to other communities, and to have someone come in to check the house when they were away (see Tables 6.3). However they were less likely to inform the police that they would be absent from their homes.

Table 6.3   Property Left Empty

'Do you normally inform neighbours or friends if you are leaving the house empty for a while, eg going on holiday?' (% replying 'yes')

	Catholic Lower Working Class Urban	Protestant Lower Working Class Urban	Mixed Middle Class Urban	Catholic Small Towns	Protestant Small Towns
Neighbours	70.2	59.3	77.3	46.9	54.5
Relatives	66.0	64.5	61.7	53.5	46.6
Friends	18.6	5.9	9.1	7.7	3.1
Police	2.9	10.0	12.2	13.6	8.9
No-one	2.9	6.9	4.3	9.8	7.2
DK/NA	6.7	9.3	1.8	14.0	9.2

'When you go out do you ensure there is someone in the house?' (This question was only asked if there was more than one person in the household.)

Always	6.6	3.7	1.3	2.0	3.2
Sometimes	10.4	1.4	1.0	2.4	6.5
Never	82.2	92.1	92.8	90.1	87.0
DK/NA	0.8	2.8	4.9	5.6	3.2

(Unweighted Data)

Overall, only a small proportion of respondents stated that they would normally inform the police that they would be away. Respondents in Catholic small towns were the most likely to do so, but even in those communities less than 14 per cent of respondents said that they would inform them. Equally, hardly any respondents stated that they would normally ask the police to check their properties in their absence. It is also significant that respondents living in Protestant small towns were least likely to have their house checked by someone in their absence, which mirrors their less marked worries about being burgled (see chapter.four).

A further precaution that people may take to secure their property is to ensure that it is never left empty. To ascertain whether this in fact occurs a further question was asked of respondents in households in which there was more than one adult resident (see Table 6.3). It was significant that some respondents stated that their properties were never left empty, and whilst there may be a variety of reasons for this, it is noticeable that it is most pronounced amongst respondents in Catholic lower working class urban communities, where respondents had expressed a greater worry about their homes being broken into (see also chapter four).

Insurance

Respondents were asked whether they had household insurance against theft, and whether they had made a claim on that policy in the last twelve months. It should be noted, however, that only 21 claims had been made, so caution needs to be taken in interpreting these results. There were however, noticeable variations between the communities as regards insurance cover. Respondents in mixed middle class communities were the most likely to have such cover, followed by those in small towns, those in Catholic lower working class urban communities and then those in Protestant lower working class urban communities. In general terms, this can be accounted for by factors concerning comparative affluence and the degree of apprehension about the possibility of a burglary. But when respondents' answers as to why they were not insured were considered, a degree of apathy was also apparent, with 38 per cent of respondents in Catholic and Protestant lower working class urban communities responding that they 'had not got around to it'[1].

Crime surveys in Britain have shown that a significant proportion of victims were not insured, 49 per cent in terms of the 1996 Scottish Crime Survey (1998, p.25) and 53 per cent in terms of the 1998 British Crime

---

[1] Respondents who were not insured in mixed middle class and Catholic and Protestant small town communities were too few in number for the purposes of statistical analysis.

Survey (1998, p.54). The Scottish Survey found that 84 per cent of respondents were insured against theft and that those without such insurance were more likely to rent their homes and to have a lower household income, and to be in social class E (1998, p.66).

Table 6.4   Home Insurance

'Are the contents of your house insured against theft?'

	Catholic Lower Working Class Urban	Protestant Lower Working Class Urban	Mixed Middle Class Urban	Catholic Small Towns	Protestant Small Towns
Yes	67.3	58.6	92.1	76.2	77.1
No	30.1	41.0	5.4	20.6	20.9
DK	2.6	0.3	2.5	3.1	2.1

(Unweighted Data)

Such profiling serves a number of purposes. It may raise potential victims' awareness of what they stand to lose without such insurance, it informs insurance companies of potential markets and it again reiterates the governmental rationality on risk/benefit analysis. Equally, in terms of those with such insurance it produces a form of 'compulsory networking' (O'Malley, 1991, p.181) in the event of their suffering a loss through the requirement that they report the incident to the police. This may be to safeguard the interests of the insurance company but it also provides information/knowledge to the police for profiling victims and communities in circumstances where the victim does not have an incentive to otherwise report the incident, either in terms of recovering their property or the police clearing the crime. The RUC Chief Constable's Report for 1998/1999, for example, has a clearance rate for burglary of 17.1 per cent (1999, p29).

Means of Reducing Crime

The final section in this part concerns respondents' views on the best means of reducing crime and improving safety in their communities. They were given a list of possible courses of action and asked to identify the three most important strategies in descending order of priority. Table 6.5 provides details of respondents' first preferences.

Apart from a wide variety of alternative suggestions, the only two strategies that drew wide support were an increase in police patrols and better facilities for young people. The latter attracted significant support from respondents in Catholic lower working class urban communities, Catholic small towns and Protestant lower working class urban communities, and to a lesser extent Protestant small towns and the middle class communities. This reflects, to a limited extent, the existing use of such facilities in the different communities, but may also be a more significant reflection of the worries expressed by the communities as regards the activities that their children may become involved in when they are not being supervised by an adult (see chapter seven). It also shows some of the general problems facing the different communities in terms of the physical environment, crime, social problems, and problems emanating from the 'troubles', in terms of how they affect the community as a whole, but also as a reflection of parental concerns for their children (see chapters two and seven).

The suggestion of increased police patrols attracted the largest support amongst mixed middle class communities (47 per cent chose it as their first preference), Protestant lower working class urban communities (41 per cent) and Protestant small towns (27 per cent). Catholic small towns and Catholic lower working class urban communities had significantly lower support for such measures, with 24 per cent of respondents in Catholic small towns and only 16 per cent of respondents in Catholic lower working class urban communities choosing it as their first preference. These figures appear to be a reflection of a number of factors; the level of concern being expressed about crime in the different communities, attitudes of mistrust towards the police; and feelings of antipathy or apathy towards the police.

When respondents' second and third preferences were analysed, the same pattern of response continued. If the 'other' category is excluded, the two dominant themes remain for more police patrols and better facilities for young people. The only other measure that attracted any significant support was 'improve appearance of the area', amongst respondents in Catholic lower working class urban communities. Here 7 per cent of respondents mentioned it as their second and third preferences respectively.

In terms of better facilities for young people, 29 per cent and 7 per cent of respondents in Catholic lower working class urban communities mentioned it as their second and third preferences respectively. The corresponding figures for Catholic small towns being 18 and 5 per cent, for Protestant lower working class urban communities 18 and 3 per cent, for mixed middle class communities 14 and 4 per cent, and for Protestant small towns 11 and 2 per cent.

Table 6.5   Reducing Crime

'What do you think are the most important things that could be done to reduce crime and improve safety around here?'

	Catholic Lower Working Class Urban	Protestant Lower Working Class Urban	Mixed Middle Class Urban	Catholic Small Towns	Protestant Small Towns
Better Lighting	1.4	1.2	1.1	3.7	1.2
Improve appearance of the area	2.7	1.8	0.2	0.8	0.3
More police patrols	15.9	41.1	46.6	23.9	26.8
Improvements in locks on doors, windows etc.	0.3	0.8	1.2	1.2	0.0
Video cameras	0.8	3.5	0.0	1.1	1.3
Better facilities for young people	33.6	26.9	15.2	29.4	17.3
Better relations between neighbours	3.4	1.5	1.2	2.7	4.1
Other	33.9	11.5	19.5	23.6	20.6
DK	8.1	11.5	14.9	14.6	26.4

(Weighted Data)

The suggestion of more police patrols continued to attract little support amongst respondents in Catholic lower working class urban communities, where 7 and 6 per cent of respondents mentioned it as their second and third preferences respectively. Amongst respondents in mixed middle class communities the corresponding figures were 9 and 3 per cent, and amongst Protestant lower working class urban communities 10 and 3 per cent. However there was a variation in the replies from respondents in Catholic and Protestant small towns. 9 per cent of respondents in Catholic small towns mentioned more police patrols as their second preference and 7 per cent as their third preference, compared to 9 and 1 per cent of respondents in Protestant small towns. This may reflect the different attitudes pertaining to policing in Catholic small towns, compared to those existing in Catholic lower working class urban communities (see chapter five).

Conclusions

At the time the Northern Ireland Community Crime Survey was carried out, it does not appear that the governmental rationality on securing the home had permeated to all of the communities contained within the survey. As the survey was not conducted on a representative sample of the population of Northern Ireland, direct comparisons cannot be made with the results obtained from surveys conducted elsewhere, such as the British Crime Survey. It does appear though, that the extent of the security measures taken within the communities constituting the survey is on a smaller scale than those taken elsewhere. Respondents in mixed middle class communities may be an exception to this pattern and be more amenable to governmental rationality, although other factors, such as greater affluence, may have predisposed them to such measures. The single most significant factor in inducing respondents to take security measures, however, was personal experience of crime, and this appeared in all of the communities contained within the survey. It would appear that risk assessment, as well as apathy, played a prominent part in deciding whether preventative measures and insurance were to be taken. This is especially marked in terms of the different responses elicited from respondents in urban and small town communities, although some of those responses may have been prompted by respondents' experiences and fears about problems emanating from the 'troubles' and sectarian attacks, particularly in Catholic lower working class communities.

If the peace process continues, and the indications that ordinary crime will increase are confirmed, then it may be expected that the situation will significantly change. The expectations of Northern Ireland enjoying a relatively low level of ordinary crime may be replaced by a greater concern and worry about ordinary crime that will produce a more conducive atmosphere for governmental rationality to be accepted, including the responsibilized or prudentialised subject. This last point also has to be considered in the context of the Patten Report, which, as will be discussed in our concluding chapter, is essentially a report on governmentality. If the Patten Report is implemented and is successful, it should have a profound effect on how policing is perceived and how it is conducted.

Respondents views in the Communities Crime Survey on their attitudes to the RUC were most marked between those in Catholic and Protestant lower working class communities, with significant variations between their contacts, experiences and perceptions of the police. When respondents were asked about the best means of reducing crime in their area, respondents in Protestant lower working class communities considered more police patrols to be the single most significant factor, and better facilities for young people the second; respondents in Catholic lower working class communities took a diametrically opposing view. For respondents in one of those communities, the police were seen as the solution to a range of problems, whilst in the other, the police were one of the problems that the communities faced. Different forms of policing, different initiatives, are therefore required by the different communities. This flexible, community-oriented approach to policing was rarely attempted under the monolithic, security focused approach to policing that has pertained to Northern Ireland. One rare exception was the Markets Neighbourhood Policing Project in Belfast that has been lauded by the Patten Report (1999, 7.6)[2].

Such approaches are inherent within a governmentality approach to policing where the state / civil society divide, and the ideological baggage that such a divide carries in Northern Ireland, disappears under the requirements to secure the most efficient cost / benefit programme to solve the problem under scrutiny. Foucault's suggestion that the forms by which power may be exercised can be seen as a triangle of 'sovereignty - discipline – government' (1991, p102) connotes a flexible, varied approach to governmentality that is inherent within the Patten Report with its insistence that decisions on policing should be taken to ensure that they are 'responsive to local community needs [rather] than directions from senior ranks far removed from the neighbourhood' (1999, 7.14). Thus, some communities may desire more direct forms of interventions as regards the problems of crime, whilst others would wish for more of a government-at-

---

[2] This was the successful implementation of a community policing project in a republican area in Belfast.

a-distance approach. The Patten report states as regards the latter approach, 'If, for example, it is discovered that there are no facilities for young people in that area, the police beat manager will have to seek help from community leaders and groups to get the matter addressed' (1999,7.17). Such an approach, if it succeeds, is not a negation of policing but an extension of governance.

Quite apart from the Patten Report, however, what should prove to be irrevocable steps have already been taken in terms of how the discourse in policing is conducted in Northern Ireland, a discourse that heavily reflects the governmentality approach. The forward to the latest Report of the Chief Constable, after noting the increased levels of ordinary crime, proceeds, 'We must therefore ensure that we make the best possible use of our own available personnel, continue to improve our management techniques, and exploit all opportunities by developments in technology.... Everyone can contribute to crime prevention and detection through taking common-sense precaution....' (1999, p.13) The body of the Report reiterates that, 'Crime prevention is one of the fundamental principles of policing... Everyone has a responsibility to take all reasonable precautions to protect their homes, businesses and property' (1999, p.23). The emphasis on the Report is on partnership with other agencies, governmental and non-governmental, on community policing, 'a wide range of multi-agency and community initiatives and programmes' (1999, p.62) and policing in partnership. Such an emphasis would have been unthinkable even a few years ago, and reflects the changed security situation and governmental rationality, and with it a new emphasis on crime prevention.

7 Children in Public Space

Introduction

This chapter explores children's safety in the public space within the communities as measured by concerns expressed by their parents. This relatively novel aspect of the survey was designed to elicit how parents feel about the dangers and risks attached to various activities that they believe their children may be involved in during their leisure time. It also explores the range of activities that parents report their children as being involved in and the way in which such activities are organised in each of the communities.

For the purpose of analysis children were placed in four age categories: under 5 years; 5-11 years; 12-15 years; and 16-17 years. Parents[1] in each of the five communities were asked to evaluate the safety and quality of their area in relation to their own concerns about their children. This involved general evaluations as well as more specific inquiries about particular concerns. The survey examines parents' viewpoints and their understandings of their children's activities as opposed to the experience of the children themselves. Parental concerns are used as an indicator of more general feelings about the quality of life within the physical and social space in the various communities.

In many ways, concerns about children and their leisure activities tap into important issues. There is, perhaps, a general sense of crisis about the idea of childhood resulting from changing patterns of family life (for example, Miles, 1994), perceived reduction in physical activity inside and outside school (for example, Cale and Almond, 1992; Armstrong and McManus, 1994), and, more generally, urban expansion, increased traffic and a range of related dangers. Much of this concern focuses on ideas of safety as well as worries that parents may have about their children coming

---

[1] The questions in this chapter were only asked of individuals with children.

to harm from a variety of sources. Such concerns are of course extremely subjective. In relative terms, they may have little to do with real risk. While the hope that life will be safe and happy for one's children is perhaps spread relatively evenly across the communities, risk from a variety of environmental factors is certainly less evenly spread and may depend on factors such as relative deprivation. However, fears about children's safety may provide a further indicator of how respondents feel about the quality of their area generally and the strength and value of their community links and ties.

The amount of freedom that parents allow their children, with regard to going out alone, is related to the issue of how particular areas are evaluated more generally. This relates directly to issues of perceived safety but also to a wide range of factors that are experienced differentially across the communities. For example, considering that the number of cars nationally has increased by 80 per cent over the last twenty years and more than 20 per cent of peak time car journeys are taking children to school (Department of Transport, 1995), there are general fears that children's free-range, informal play space and opportunity is being restricted. However, the impact of such fears will vary across economic groups and across the urban/rural distinction.

Issues about the degree of parental freedom also connect with feelings of ownership and civic holding that parents and children may have over the public space in and around their community. In 1990 it was suggested that 'the personal freedom and choice permitted a typical seven year old in 1971 are not now permitted until children reach the age of about nine and a half' (Hillman *et al.*, 1990). There are a range of factors involved in such curtailing of children's freedom and it is clear that the 'typical' child of this Policy Studies Institute study is, in the communities examined here, made up from a very wide range of different experiences. The permission granted to children to go out alone, either during the day or at night, is, across the various communities examined within the survey, permission to go into extremely different environments. Ideas of protective parents, safe and accommodating home environments, opportunities and necessities as well as a whole range of different potential dangers are in practice factored into a complex pattern where social class and the urban/rural divide combine to suggest a degree of complexity that denies the possibility of there being a 'typical' child controlled by his or her parents on the basis of a simple, rational decision. The very different environments and opportunities within the various communities provide significantly different choices for parents and this is reflected in the data.

This complex picture of what parents allow, and its relationship to their feelings of safety, also connects with ideas of citizenship and participation in the public space that belongs to the communities. The rights of children to leisure and to play, and to meet with others and associate, are enshrined in international law via the United Nations Convention on the Rights of the Child 1989. A number of good practice guides for planners and for local councils have been developed (e.g. Wheway and Millward, 1997). Indeed, Belfast City Council are currently drawing up a draft 'Play Policy' (Belfast City Council, 1999). However, it is clear that these rights, and any sense of civic belonging or ownership of public space, are experienced and enjoyed in very different ways across the communities. Public space is physically different in the various communities and it is certainly experienced differently. Its use engenders a range of differing worries and concerns within the various communities, and this may effect not just general measures of satisfaction with an area but deeper feelings about a sense of community.

This idea of how the different communities experience an idea of 'community' is followed up beyond its connection with public space and into ideas of civic society. Northern Ireland is often depicted as a society which has particularly firm family ties and strong networks from civil society and the Church. Indeed, as mentioned earlier, such factors have been given as explanations for what is seen as a low rate of ordinary crime (Morison and Geary, 1989). It is important to interrogate closely these oracular claims of common knowledge and at the same time examine wider concerns that childhood activities may have become increasingly organised, perhaps in response to fears about safety with free-range play. Ideas of the privatisation of play and leisure or even of the 'commodification of childhood' are explored in questions that address the issue of where exactly children spend their after-school time.

General Evaluations of Children's Safety

Respondents were asked to evaluate how good the area they live in is with regard to bringing up children, in comparison with most other areas in Northern Ireland. There is a noticeable distinction between the evaluations of those living in mixed middle class areas, Catholic small towns, Protestant small towns and those living in Catholic or Protestant urban areas. In the lower working class areas, both Catholic and Protestant, far fewer saw their area as better (only 12 and 11 per cent respectively) compared to 64 per cent in the mixed middle class urban area. Small towns, both Catholic and Protestant, were more positive again with 73 and 87 per cent respectively seeing their area as better than others for bringing up children. More respondents from Protestant lower working class areas (71 per cent) saw their area as about the same as others in Northern Ireland than respondents in Catholic lower working class areas (54 per cent). Relatively few respondents in mixed middle class areas or small towns evaluated their areas as worse than others in Northern Ireland, but 15 per cent of Protestant lower working class respondents and 34 per cent of Catholic lower working class respondents expressed the view that their area was a worse place to bring up children than elsewhere in Northern Ireland (Table 7.1).

Table 7.1   Good Area to Bring Up Children

'How good is this area to bring up children compared with elsewhere in Northern Ireland?'

	Catholic Lower Working Class Urban	Protestant Lower Working Class Urban	Mixed Middle Class Urban	Catholic Small Towns	Protestant Small Towns
Better	12.3	11.0	64.1	72.6	86.5
About the same	53.8	71.2	30.5	23.4	10.4
Worse	34.0	15.1	3.1	2.4	2.1
D/K	0.0	2.7	2.3	1.6	1.0

The quality of living space issues and perceptions of the environment in which respondents live that were explored in chapter two (see Tables 2.2-2.8) are, in part, reproduced in the evaluations of children's safety. Between about 50 to 60 per cent of parents allowed their children out alone to play. These generally higher levels of concern about disorder and crime problems in lower working class urban communities are reproduced in feelings about children's safety.

This general evaluation of children's safety was followed up by more specific inquiries about children's recreation. Parents were questioned about how safe they felt their children (in various age categories) were when playing outside by themselves. Generally, there was most concern for children in the under-5 year old group, especially for those in the Catholic lower working class urban areas. About 30 per cent of parents from Catholic lower working class areas felt that their under five year old children were either 'not very safe' or 'not at all safe', while only 8 per cent of parents of under five year old children in Protestant lower working class areas, 6 per cent in mixed middle class areas, 4 per cent in Catholic small towns and 14 per cent in Protestant small towns shared the same level of concern for their safety.

Table 7.2   Children's Safety

'How Safe Do You Think Your Children Are When They Go Out To Play By Themselves?

	Catholic Lower Working Class Urban	Protestant Lower Working Class Urban	Mixed Middle Class Urban	Catholic Small Towns	Protestant Small Towns
Very safe					
Under 5	15.0	15.4	17.6	37.5	28.6
5-11	26.5	24.2	22.2	58.9	46.7
12-15	25.0	31.8	15.2	57.1	59.1
Fairly safe					
Under 5	55.0	61.5	70.6	29.2	28.6
5-11	57.1	60.6	71.1	35.7	43.3
12-15	70.0	54.5	84.8	31.4	40.9
Not very safe					
Under 5	20.0	0.0	5.9	4.2	0.0
5-11	14.3	9.1	4.4	5.4	10.0
12-15	5.0	9.1	0.0	8.6	0.0
Not all safe					
Under 5	10.0	7.7	0.0	0.0	14.3
5-11	2.0	6.1	2.2	0.0	0.0
12-15	0.0	0.0	0.0	0.0	0.0
D/K					
Under 5	0.0	15.4	5.9	29.2	28.6
5-11	0.0	0.0	0.0	0.0	0.0
12-15	0.0	4.5	0.0	2.9	0.0

There was a slightly higher evaluation of safety for the 5-11 year old age group and a higher again rating for the 12-15 age category. Indeed, *all* those in the Protestant small towns and in the mixed middle class urban areas felt that their children in the 12-15 year old age group were either 'fairly safe' or 'very safe' when outside by themselves. In the Catholic lower working class areas, the figure for those that felt their children were 'not very safe' or 'not at all safe' fell to only 5 per cent in relation to the 12-15 year old group, which is even lower than in the Protestant lower working class areas and in the Catholic small towns (Table 7.2).

Table 7.3   Allowing Children Out Alone – Day/Night

'Do you allow your children out to school or the shop alone?'

	Catholic Lower Working Class Urban	Protestant Lower Working Class Urban	Mixed Middle Class Urban	Catholic Small Towns	Protestant Small Towns
DAY					
Yes					
Under 5	12.8	6.7	0.0	0.0	2.8
5-11	53.6	62.8	55.7	64.5	53.5
12-15	89.6	100.0	94.2	95.3	94.3
No					
Under 5	87.2	93.3	100.0	93.9	97.2
5-11	46.4	37.2	44.3	35.5	46.7
12-15	10.4	0.0	5.8	4.7	5.7
NIGHT					
Yes					
Under 5	2.6	0.0	3.4	0.0	0.0
5-11	15.9	20.9	8.2	14.5	13.3
12-15	64.6	79.3	42.3	65.1	62.9
No					
Under 5	97.4	100.0	96.6	93.9	100.0
5-11	84.1	79.1	91.8	85.5	86.7
12-15	35.4	20.7	57.7	34.9	37.1

Table 7.4 Extent of Worry when Children are Outside

'Do you worry about (your children) when they are out alone (without an adult)?'

	Catholic Lower Working Class Urban	Protestant Lower Working Class Urban	Mixed Middle Class Urban	Catholic Small Towns	Protestant Small Towns
A lot					
Under 5	15.4	6.7	5.2	10.2	5.6
5-11	23.2	25.6	1.6	10.5	11.1
12-15	29.2	20.7	11.5	11.6	8.6
16-17	31.3	27.3	7.4	15.8	10.5
Quite a lot					
Under 5	48.7	6.7	8.6	2.0	5.6
5-11	49.3	30.2	31.1	11.8	8.9
12-15	37.5	34.5	28.8	14.0	5.7
16-17	31.3	9.1	29.6	15.8	10.5
A little					
Under 5	5.1	3.3	3.4	6.1	2.8
5-11	13.0	18.6	39.3	26.3	26.7
12-15	20.8	31.0	50.0	39.5	34.3
16-17	18.8	18.2	59.3	21.1	26.3
Not at all					
Under 5	0.0	0.0	3.4	8.2	0.0
5-11	10.1	9.3	9.8	35.5	24.4
12-15	10.4	13.8	7.7	27.9	45.7
16-17	18.8	45.5	3.7	42.1	47.4
Not allowed out					
Under 5	23.1	83.3	79.3	71.4	83.3
5-11	4.3	16.3	18.0	15.8	28.9
12-15	2.1	0.0	1.9	7.0	5.7
16-17	0.0	0.0	0.0	5.3	5.3
D/K					
Under 5	7.7	0.0	0.0	2.0	2.8
5-11	0.0	0.0	0.0	0.0	0.0
12-15	0.0	0.0	0.0	0.0	0.0
16-17	0.0	0.0	0.0	0.0	0.0

In particular, parents were asked if they allowed their children in the various age categories to go out alone, for example, to the local shop, either during the day or at night. A more protective attitude towards under 5 year old children was universal, although 13 per cent of children under 5 years old were allowed out alone during the day in Catholic lower working class areas. This is in comparison to only 7 per cent in Protestant lower working class areas, 3 per cent in the Protestant small towns, and none at all in the mixed middle class communities or the Catholic small towns. Parents in the mixed middle class urban areas were generally the most protective, although 3 per cent apparently allowed their under 5 year olds to go out alone after dark. Children from both the 5-11 year old groups and the 12-15 year old categories in the Protestant lower working class were afforded the most freedom to go out alone by day and at night (Table 7.3).

Parents were asked about the degree of worry that they have when their children are out alone without an adult. Parents of children in the 16-17 year old age bracket were included here. Worry was reported as being greater in the urban areas than in small towns. Those in the Catholic lower working class areas expressed most worry with more than 60 per cent of parents in all age groups (73 per cent for the 5-11 years group) reporting that they worried 'a lot' or 'quite a lot'. Small towns reported least worry, as is consistent with their more general fears of crime (chapter four). Parents in the other areas expressed significantly less worry (Table 7.4).

Again, the more general concerns relating to perceptions of the communities that are discussed in chapter two are reflected in the levels of concern that parents in the various areas express. It is interesting, however, that worry about those in the 12-17 year old age bracket out alone does not correlate directly with concerns expressed in Table 7.4 (above) relating to the problem of teenagers having little to do. Those expressing 'a lot' or 'quite a lot' of concern for teenagers in both the Catholic lower working class communities (64 per cent) and the Protestant lower working class communities (46 per cent) are matched by relatively high percentages identifying little for teenagers to do as a 'big' problem in their area (64 and 56 per cent respectively). However, although more than 60 per cent of respondents in the small towns identify little for teenagers to do as a 'big' problem, relatively fewer express 'a lot' or 'quite a lot' of worry about the safety of their teenagers (29 per cent for Catholic small towns and 18 per cent for Protestant small towns). In the mixed middle class areas, only 18 per cent see little for teenagers to do as a 'big problem' but almost 40 per cent express 'a lot' or 'quite a lot' of worry about their teenage children. This, perhaps, not only reinforces ideas of a more protective middle class ethos but also indicates how middle class fears are more attuned to the idea of something happening to their children rather than their children actively getting themselves into trouble. Below, the exploration of particular parental concerns develops this view of how fears and dangers are experienced differently, depending on the type of community in which respondents live.

Particular Parental Concerns

Questions were asked about particular worries that parents may have had with regard to their children. The list of concerns was similar but not identical to those used in the Scottish Crime Survey (Scottish Office, 1998).

The Communities Crime Survey found that worries were markedly higher in the urban areas, particularly in the lower working class communities which consistently reported higher levels of 'a lot' or 'quite a lot' of worry. Parents of children in the 5-11 year old age group expressed the greatest worry about their children being run over by motor vehicles but, for those parents in lower working class areas, worries about playing in dangerous places came a close second. Worries about bullying by other children and being sexually molested featured next in the list of concerns. Worries about theft figured more strongly in lower working class communities than in middle class or small town areas. Worries about children actively getting into trouble themselves (as contrasted with events happening to them) were markedly higher in the lower working class communities, as were worries relating to the police and paramilitaries (Table 7.5).

Table 7.6 shows the particular worries that concern parents with children in the 12-16 age group. Some anxieties seem to have receded with, for example, worry about motor vehicles much reduced. Worry about playing in dangerous places remains high in Catholic lower working class communities. Worry about children being sexually molested or hit or bullied by adults is particularly high in lower working class areas and Catholic communities. Worries about activities that are instigated by children (in contrast to adults' actions that impinge upon children) increase too. Drugs and alcohol provide a source of worry for all parents but particularly for those in Catholic lower working class areas where four out of ten parents express 'a lot' or 'quite a lot' of worry about drinking alcohol and more than half of those questioned worry about drugs (Table 7.6).

Table 7.5 Particular Worries

Do You Worry About the Possibility Of The Following Specific Things When They Are Out Alone (Without A Responsible Adult)?

	Catholic Lower Working Class Urban	Protestant Lower Working Class Urban	Mixed Middle Class Urban	Catholic Small Towns	Protestant Small Towns
5-11					
Playing in dangerous places	79.7	72.1	49.2	55.2	42.3
Being run over by motor vehicles	86.9	81.4	70.5	59.2	55.5
Bullied by other children	63.7	65.2	39.3	47.4	33.3
Being a nuisance to other people	39.1	46.5	29.5	19.7	31.1
Playing truant from school	17.4	13.9	4.9	7.8	4.4
Involved with drugs/glue sniffing	36.2	28.0	18.0	18.4	22.2
Having things stolen from them	21.7	25.6	9.8	10.6	13.3
Being sexually molested	47.8	51.1	39.4	30.3	26.7
Hit or bullied by adults	30.4	25.6	13.1	18.4	13.3
Attacked by dogs	33.3	27.2	27.9	23.7	15.6
Getting into fights with other youngsters	31.9	41.9	14.7	18.4	8.9
Vandalising property	18.8	27.9	6.5	6.5	8.9
Drinking Alcohol	21.7	20.9	6.6	7.8	8.8
Getting into trouble with police	15.9	23.3	4.9	5.2	8.8
Hassled by police	15.9	16.3	4.9	5.2	0.0
Joining gangs	20.2	30.2	3.3	5.2	4.4
Getting involved with paramilitaries	21.7	25.6	3.3	3.9	4.4
Hassled by paramilitaries	20.3	21.0	3.3	3.9	0.0

Table 7.6   Particular Worries

'Do You Worry About The Possibility Of The Following Specific Things When They Are Out Alone (Without A Responsible Adult)?'

12-16	Catholic Lower Working Class Urban	Protestant Lower Working Class Urban	Mixed Middle Class Urban	Catholic Small Towns	Protestant Small Towns
Playing in dangerous places	72.9	37.9	38.5	34.9	20.0
Being run over by motor vehicles	62.5	41.4	34.7	34.9	34.2
Bullied by other children	56.3	34.4	25.0	32.5	34.3
Being a nuisance to other people	41.7	34.5	17.3	21.0	20.0
Playing truant from school	27.1	20.7	9.6	7.0	11.5
Involved with drugs/glue sniffing	56.3	41.4	30.8	41.9	34.3
Having things stolen from them	37.5	24.1	17.3	9.3	14.3
Being sexually molested	58.4	55.2	36.5	25.6	25.7
Hit or bullied by adults	50.0	37.9	19.2	11.7	17.2
Attacked by dogs	39.6	31.0	17.3	16.3	5.7
Getting into fights with other youngsters	35.5	24.1	9.6	18.6	8.6
Vandalising property	37.5	17.2	5.7	9.4	8.6
Drinking Alcohol	41.7	27.6	13.4	27.9	20.0
Getting into trouble with police	31.3	20.7	13.5	14.0	8.6
Hassled by police	37.5	13.8	7.6	7.0	8.6
Joining gangs	41.7	27.5	13.5	16.3	5.8
Getting involved with paramilitaries	37.5	34.5	13.4	16.3	8.6
Hassled by paramilitaries	33.3	24.1	11.6	11.7	2.9

Another interesting finding is that most communities report emphatically that the cease-fires made no difference to their level of worry about their children. However, it is startling that this figure falls to 39 per cent for Catholic lower working class communities where more than 54 per cent declared that they worried less during the cease-fires. It is interesting to speculate on whether this is reflective of the impact that the cease-fires had on feelings of safety or of a more general positive feeling engendered during that time which is marked retrospectively by feelings of increased safety (Table 7.7).

Table 7.7   Worry During Cease-fires

Did You Worry More or Less About Your Children During The Cease-fires?

	Catholic Lower Working Class Urban	Protestant Lower Working Class Urban	Mixed Middle Class Urban	Catholic Small Towns	Protestant Small Towns
More	3.8	2.7	0.0	0.0	2.1
Less	54.7	19.2	25.2	8.9	8.3
No difference	38.7	78.1	74.0	90.3	89.6
OK	2.8	0.0	0.8	0.8	0.0

Children's Activities: Family and Civil Society

To explore further the often quoted notion that Northern Ireland society is particularly family and community oriented, questions were addressed as to the involvement of children in certain activities. The range of alternatives offered was larger than those used in the Scottish Crime Survey, although, of course, both the methodology and research questions differ in the two studies (Scottish Office, 1998: page 97). Table 7.8 shows the responses given to questions about the out-of-school hours activities (including school-based activities) in which children are involved. It is striking that church-organised activities, while important, particularly for the younger age group, are much less popular in Catholic communities (both urban and small town) than in Protestant communities or in mixed urban areas. Sports clubs and leisure centres are generally popular in a fairly even pattern across the communities, but in Catholic urban areas they were the most popular with more than 70 per cent of parents saying that their 12-15 year olds used these facilities.

There is little evidence, even in mixed middle class areas, that childhood activities are privatised to any great extent; privately organised and funded activities are used most in Protestant small towns and least in Catholic urban areas. Public space is less popular than friends' houses everywhere but in urban working class areas. To an extent, in small towns, local public space is a popular forum for meeting friends. Public space in middle class areas is used much less. Overall it is public space in the immediate local community that is used rather than the city centre or shopping centre.

The details here may be of assistance in helping to explore the often quoted notion that Northern Ireland society is particularly family and community oriented. Although there seems to be much less church organised activities in both the Catholic urban and small town communities, elsewhere church-centred activities do figure significantly. This is particularly true of the Protestant lower working class communities where church activities exceed even visiting friends' houses as the most popular activity for the younger age group (in Catholic communities, the church involvement may be relatively lower with regard to organising leisure activities but this may have to be placed beside the continuing role of the church in education and in other areas). There is some indication that public space, particularly for the older age group, is an important arena for social intercourse, although this is not uniform throughout the communities. Catholic urban and Catholic and Protestant small towns report a higher incidence of mixing with friends in public places in their own area than do Protestant urban communities and, particularly, the mixed middle class communities. This is so despite higher levels of satisfaction with their area as a good place to bring up children (Table 7.1 above).

Evaluations of safety relating to children out alone (Table 7.2) or expressions about particular worries relating to the physical environment, or interference from adults or other children or gangs (see Tables 7.5 and 7.6), do not correlate closely with the actual activities that children are involved in, as reported by their parents. While respondents in lower working class communities, particularly Catholic ones, express more concern about such dangers, their use of public space in their own area, as opposed to the presumably safer private space of friends' houses or organised activities, remains quite high.

Table 7.8   Activities out of School Hours

	Catholic Lower Working Class Urban	Protestant Lower Working Class Urban	Mixed Middle Class Urban	Catholic Small Towns	Protestant Small Towns
Sports clubs / leisure centres					
5-11	42.0	18.6	45.9	48.7	42.2
12-15	70.8	41.4	57.7	51.2	51.4
School activities					
5-11	27.5	18.6	29.5	17.1	31.1
12-15	39.6	34.5	51.9	18.6	31.4
Community organised activities and clubs					
5-11	36.2	14.0	11.5	46.1	26.7
12-15	45.8	6.9	9.6	55.8	22.9
Church organised activities and clubs					
5-11	14.5	67.4	42.6	11.8	40.0
12-15	12.5	34.5	23.1	16.3	31.4
Privately organised and funded activities					
5-11	4.3	14.0	13.1	19.7	20.0
12-15	4.2	0.0	15.4	7.0	20.0
Visiting friends houses					
5-11	60.9	51.2	50.8	60.5	62.2
12-15	58.3	55.2	40.4	60.5	60.0
Mixing with friends in public places in this area					
5-11	56.5	41.9	21.3	52.6	42.2
12-15	60.4	37.9	28.8	58.1	62.9
Mixing with friends in public places in other areas					
5-11	4.3	4.7	3.3	9.2	13.3
12-15	18.8	17.2	7.7	16.3	28.6

Of course, much of the explanation for this may lie with the traditional use of public space such as the street and neighbourhood as a forum for children's play and the relative absence of spacious houses and gardens for children to play in plus the absence of funds to engage in other activities or visit public space in other areas. While similar considerations may apply in Protestant lower working class communities, the pattern of use of public space, particularly for those in the 12-15 year old age bracket is much less, with only mixed middle class areas reporting less use.

Conclusions

This chapter explores evaluations of safety as measured by concerns expressed by parents about their children as they fall within four age categories.

Respondents living in mixed middle class areas and in small towns evaluated their communities more favourably as an area to bring up children compared with those living in Catholic or Protestant working class communities. While more than 70 per cent of those in Protestant working class communities saw their area as about the same as others in Northern Ireland, only 54 per cent of those in Catholic working class communities took a similar view while 34 per cent (more than twice as many as in other communities) saw their area as a worse place to bring up children.

Generally, the least concern was expressed for the safety of older children. However, a considerable degree of unease was expressed about the safety of those under 5 years old, particularly in the Catholic lower working class areas where 30 per cent felt that their children were either 'not very safe' or 'not at all safe'. 14 per cent of those in Protestant small towns registered a similar view, but the figure was below 10 per cent in the other areas. Concerns for the 5-11 year old age bracket were highest in the Catholic and Protestant lower working class areas, but not far behind in the Protestant small towns. Children in the 12-15 year old age range were generally perceived to be safer and indeed in the mixed middle class areas and the Protestant small towns there were no respondents who believed their children to be either 'not very safe' or 'not at all safe'.

Parents were asked particularly if they allowed their children in the various age categories to go out alone, for example to the local shop either during the day or at night. A more protective attitude towards under 5 year old children was universal. Parents in the mixed middle class urban areas were generally the most protective while children from both the 5-11 years and the 12-15 years category were allowed more freedom by both day and night. However, more than 30 per cent of children between 12 and 15 years (and more than half in the mixed middle class areas) were not allowed out alone after dark. The degree of worry that parents felt when their children were out alone without an adult was greater in urban areas than in small towns. Worry was greatest in the Catholic lower working class communities, even for the 16-17 year age bracket.

Most communities report that the cease-fires made no difference to their level of worry. However, in Catholic lower working class communities, 58 per cent report that they worried less about their children during this period.

Questions about specific worries that parents may have regarding their children showed that concern was markedly higher in the urban areas and highest in the lower working class communities. Parents of children in the 5-11 years age group expressed the greatest worry about their children being run over by motor vehicles but, for those parents in lower working class areas, worries about playing in dangerous places came a close second, with worries about bullying by other children and being sexually molested featuring next most strongly. For children in the 12-16 years bracket, some anxieties, for example about motor vehicles, were reduced but other worries, about children being sexually molested or hit or bullied by adults, increased. These were particularly high in lower working class areas, both Catholic and Protestant, and in Catholic small towns. Drugs and alcohol provide a source of worry for all parents but particularly those in Catholic lower working class communities. The police, paramilitaries and gangs also feature strongly in the concerns of these parents.

The sorts of activities that children in different age ranges are engaged in was explored. For some communities, particularly the Protestant and mixed middle classes, church activities were prominent - especially with the younger age range. Surprisingly, in Catholic communities, the church took a small role while leisure centres and sports clubs were particularly important in Catholic lower working class areas. Public space is less popular than friends' houses everywhere but in urban working class areas, and to a lesser extent in small towns, public space in the local area is important, notwithstanding higher worries about safety there.

8 Governmentality, Communities and Crime

The survey upon which this book is based shows very clearly that there are more than the 'imagined' two communities of Protestants and Catholics in Northern Ireland. This is not to underestimate the significance of religious and political differences in constructing people's attitudes to crime, policing and the other issues considered in this book. As Anderson (1991) has argued, the ways in which communities are 'imagined' may be at least as important as their material reality. What we have attempted to do here is to offer a more substantial account of a range of *communities*, differentiated in various ways according to class, religion, locale and other factors. Each of these communities, and the individuals within them, have a diverse range of experiences and attitudes to crime and policing as well as to a whole range of other related issues.

All attempts to address problems of crime and policing in Northern Ireland should take account of such divisions and differences. Accounts which approach the issues on the basis of there being simply only two communities are too simplistic and reductionist[1]. Furthermore, wittingly or unwittingly, they contribute to a discourse which obfuscates rather than clarifies, by conflating what are many very different experiences and attitudes into an idealised, 'averaged-up citizen' who is differentiated only into broad categories of Protestant and Catholic, Nationalist and Unionist, etc. Indeed, it is possible to see this idea of an 'averaged-up citizen' within the context of broader discourses concerned with conflict management, the marginalisation of extremism and the legitimation of the state. Such discourses may be viewed as reflective of what has been referred to as a

---

[1] For example, the Patten Report (1999) refers to an idea that 'perceptions and experiences of policing can differ greatly between the two communities' (section 3:4). However, despite this initial stance, the Report develops a flexibility and adaptability in terms of suggesting controls for the police that take into account local community requirements that go beyond the simple two communities approach.

state in 'conflict mode' (McEvoy and Gormally, 1997). In such a settings it has been argued that the state may develop a range of strategies to minimise perceptions of the severity of the conflict and to offer an alternate 'vision of normality' which accentuates perceptions of social cohesion (Mulcahy, 1999). Crime surveys and surveys on policing which take place while a state is in 'conflict mode' may well be interpreted within such a paradigm.

As Northern Ireland looks at the possibilities that are promised in a future where the widespread political conflict may be replaced by new political institutions and new beginnings may seem possible, it is important to remember that many of the differences and divides within the communities that make up the post-conflict society will remain. The changed circumstances too present new and different challenges and this survey provides an indication of the depth and range of the multiple problems, which to varying degrees confront the different communities. Radical approaches are required for those problems that persist after cease-fires and settlements and the fresh issues that will arise in the changing circumstances. Prominent amongst these will be problems of crime, safety and policing. As was raised in the Introduction (chapter one), an important step has already been taken by the publication of the Patten Report (1999) which marks, we maintain, a radical shift in approach to crime and policing. This shift in emphasis can be examined in the context of recent writings on Foucault's notion of 'governmentality' and its relationship to criminology.

Crime, Safety and Governmentality

Garland (1997) has argued that already in Britain there has been a shift in governmental rationalities as regards crime and that this can be examined in the context of the governmentality literature.

Essentially this literature engages with Foucault's efforts at theorising forms of governance - or governable places - which exist outside the immediate view or interest of the state. Within criminology this approach has moved the discipline from looking predominately at 'docile bodies' as objects for the inscription of power and towards examining the complicated linkages connecting the various forms of state and non-state governance (Smandych, 1999). The governmentality approach has indeed made a mark across a whole range of social science research (see, for example, Barry *et al.* 1996; Davidson, 1997; O'Farrell, 1997; Pavlich, 1996). All of this work engages with the idea that, as Hunt and Wickham (1994) observe, there were dramatic changes in techniques of government developed in the western world from the eighteenth century onwards. As they see it, within Foucault's approach 'modernity …is marked by the emergence of "government" and "governmentality"'. Foucault is deploying 'the term "government" in a very different sense from the conventional idea of state executives and legislatures' and in a way that is consistent with his downgrading of the importance of the state' (1994, p.52). Indeed, for Foucault, government is 'not a matter of imposing laws on men, but rather of disposing the laws themselves as tactics' (Foucault, 1991, p.95). Foucault refers to 'a range of multiform tactics' for the government of populations outside of the state, as well as 'the governmentalisation of the state' itself (1991, p.95 and 101). As a result, Foucault sees the 'art of government' addressing questions of 'how to govern oneself, how to be governed, how to govern others, by whom the people will accept to be governed, and how to become the best possible governor' (1991, p.87).

All of this involves a shift away from mainly social and legal forms of reasoning and towards approaches to governance where economic factors are the dominant issue, not simply in terms of financial constraints, but also in terms of the analytical language that is employed, the objectives of policy, and the means by which policies are monitored. The language that is employed becomes one of risks and rewards, choice and cost/benefit analysis. The objectives become risk limitation, compensation and economic efficiency, and policies are subject to audits, market competition and devolved management. The idea of crime as an aberration from the norm, an abnormality to be eradicated by government intervention, has thus largely been superseded by an acceptance of crime as an existing and normal social fact. As Garland puts it, crime has 'gradually become a standard background feature of our lives - a taken for granted element of late modernity' (Garland, 1996, p.446). Crime is an everyday factor of social life, even if its effects are disproportionately shared. As such it is there to be dealt with in the same manner as other risks attached to ordinary life, such as unemployment and ill-health, by minimising the risks of it occurring and mitigating its effects should it occur. This, it is argued, is to be achieved by an increased emphasis on securing the home and insurance for the householder, enhanced measures to secure safety in public space through such means as better street lighting and neighbourhood watch schemes to greater supervision of children as well as the provision of more secured - controlled environments. Through these measures it is intended to invoke what Garland terms a *'responsibilization strategy'* (1996, p.452) and O'Malley terms *'prudentialism'* (1992, p.257; 1996, p.199).

The state and state agencies, such as the police, the criminal justice system and social services, cannot, by themselves, be expected to prevent or control crime (indeed, the manifest failure of previous policies has demonstrated this). Within this new thinking the state must require the active co-operation and partnership of numerous non-governmental organisations and individuals in order to achieve the aim of managing crime. For example, car manufacturers and the construction industry must be compelled to produce more secure products, town planners to devise safer localities, and individuals to take greater responsibility for their own security. Rather than a negation of governmental powers and responsibility, however, such a process involves an extension of power by diffusing it through a myriad of networks and actors down to the responsible or prudent citizen in order to influence his or her conduct.

Thus it is argued there is to be a partnership or co-operation between the individual and government agencies - notably the police - that invokes a new rationality of crime and policing. No longer are the police to be perceived as a bulwark against a rising tide of crime, but instead as being one of a number of government and private agencies who are concerned with possessing knowledge and expertise on managing crime. Information can be provided on local crime rates, advice can be given on the best means of securing the home and marking property so that it may be more easily recoverable should it be stolen, and of the importance of having property insurance (O'Malley, 1991). Once empowered the individual subject can then come to an autonomous decision as regards their own security and that of their family, both within their own home and their community. 'Rather than having a uniform level of security provided by the state, skilled and self-reliant individuals may now work with their peers in the "community", make arrangements with "their" police to provide the service they require and purchase the level of commodified security they deem appropriate to their specific needs' (O'Malley, 1996 p.202).

Such decisions are dependent on risk analysis and risk management - 'actuarialism'. This notion originally stemmed from calculating the risks attached to commercial enterprises and then in the early twentieth century emerged again in state concerns about managing unemployment in the labour market and the subsequent introduction of national insurance and social security systems (Hacking, 1990; 1991). Over the past twenty years, however, there has been the 'partial transformation of socialised actuarialism into privatised actuarialism (or *'prudentialism'*) as an effect of political interventions promoting the increased play of market forces' (O'Malley, 1992, p.257). If security against crime cannot be aspired to for everyone, then like other scarce commodities that have not been subject to government control, security becomes subject to market forces. Individual subjects are required to take responsibility for insurance and risk management. This of course produces inequality between those who can afford their own security and those who cannot.

In such a process, whereby responsibility is diffused throughout society, it operates in terms of governmentality on two levels: it is conducive to promoting the prudent householder *and* also acts as a deterrent against crime. Both the householder and the criminal are increasingly perceived as being rational subjects, calculating on a cost/benefit analysis their respective activities. The supposed biological, psychological and sociological traits that were once thought to identify *homo criminalis* disappear in the manifestation of *homo economicus* (Gordon, 1991, p.43). This is a being who is both rational and calculating in terms of the risks and the potential gains and costs involved in the criminal endeavour, but who can also be manipulated through his or her environment. Much of the impetus for this approach stems from work by Becker (1968) and other early economic analysts of crime and crime prevention, and more recently by van Dijk (1994), but it had previously been the subject of analysis by Foucault in the formation of his ideas about governmentality (Gordon, 1991, p.43).

Around these ideas have developed a number of criminological theories that Garland has described as 'the new criminologies of everyday life' (1996, p.450; see also Smandych, 1999). These include rational choice theory, routine activity theory, crime as opportunity and situational crime prevention theory. What these theories share is a common view of crime as being a normal everyday event that can never be eliminated, but which can only be better managed. More traditional approaches to governing crime through the police response to criminal incidents and the use of the criminal justice system continue, but there is now a much stronger emphasis on preventing crime, reducing the fear of crime, improving public safety and raising the public's awareness of their responsibility for ensuring their own safety through security measures.

As a result of this, new technologies and expertise have developed to implement and manage crime prevention programmes and new actors are incorporated into a network of crime prevention measures. Central to this strategy is the attempt to ensure that all the agencies, communities and individuals who are in a position to contribute to these crime-reducing ends come to see it as being in their interests to do so. 'Government' is thus extended and enhanced '...in the space between the state and the offender' (Garland, 1997, p.188). While individuals or indeed communities may opt in or out of this project, by working with and through the actors involved, the overall aim is to seek or align the actors' objectives with those of the authorities: 'to make them active partners in the business of security and crime control' (1997, p.187).

Such an 'active partnership' raises particular problems in Northern Ireland, however, due to the different communities' responsiveness to governmental rationality. As this Survey shows, there are different attitudes to the state and very different ideas about what it should be responsible for within the various communities[2]. Such difficulties include at least the following.

Firstly, we would argue strongly that the 'lived differences' between communities which are clearly evident from our results must inform attempts at forming such partnerships. In practice, for example, this means that partnerships in some working class communities must involve Republicans and Loyalists, as well as those with less extreme political aspirations. This is because the 'imagined' communities of political moderates who are generally supportive of state institutions do not always correspond to the realties of diversity and variation found in this Survey.

---

[2] *Homo economicus* may be intended to embrace Republican and Loyalist, Nationalist and Unionist. But of course generally individuals do not act against what they perceive to be in their own best interests - however irrational such a calculation may seem from the outside. There may still be opposition and resistance to governmental rationality. This may manifest itself both in terms of subjects being inclined or otherwise to act as willing actors under governmental rationality and their disposition towards accepting changes in what they perceive as being governmental responsibilities, particularly as they relate to policing and security.

Indeed, partnerships in local communities cannot be forged solely with those individuals or elements of a community who correspond with the 'imagined community'. Such a strategy of excluding those perceived as extreme or antagonistic is reflective of 'conflict mode' engagement with local communities. Rather, the changed circumstances require engagement with *all* individuals and groups who are truly representative of their communities.

Secondly, all of those working for state institutions must now recognise that their legitimacy as representatives of that state cannot be assumed as axiomatic in all communities. In some communities the legitimacy of state services will be uncritically accepted. For example, in working class Protestant communities, we have suggested that the very high levels of approval for the RUC was intimately bound up with notions of political loyalty and allegiance to the state. Conversely, the problematic relationship with the RUC in lower working Class Catholic communities was intertwined with their lack of perceived legitimacy. The key point, in any new dispensation therefore, is for state institutions to recognise that legitimacy is not a given but that it is something which needs to be earned and developed through such mechanisms as 'active partnerships'.

Thirdly, given the increased fragmentation and 'hollowing out' of the modern state, active partnership requires a willingness to establish a range of different styles to relationships to suit differing communities (Morison, 2000). For example, state agencies cannot assume that in every partnership they will be a 'lead agency' in that relationship with community groups or individuals. One of the consequences of the Northern Ireland conflict has been the emergence of a strong and active civil society in local communities. In many such communities assumptions about hierarchies of power and influence by state agencies are unlikely to lead to effective partnerships. Relationships need to build upon such community strengths rather than being viewed as competing or challenging loci of power or influence.

Finally, 'active partnerships' with local communities in Northern Ireland will need to be measured not simply in areas which correspond most closely with the 'imagined communities' of the conflict. For example, the apparent acceptance or perceived legitimacy of state institutions in mixed middle class communities or small towns should not be used as the benchmark by which the state's capacity for partnership is appropriately measured. That is altogether too easy. Rather, it is in the 'hard' communities, the places in which the state/community and individual relationship has been most problematic, which are the most appropriate places to serve as a litmus test for the new dispensations.

With these issues in mind the challenges facing the new Northern Ireland in developing active partnerships between the Government institutions, communities and civil society are formidable. Perhaps one of the key documents in analysing attempts at forging a new and active partnership is the Patten Report (1999) on the future of policing in Northern Ireland.

Communities, Patten and Crime

Generally speaking the notion of governmentality has been considered up to now in relation to developments in Great Britain. In Northern Ireland more immediate issues relating to 'the troubles' have overshadowed any development of such approaches within this context. Now, however, with the Patten Report on policing there can be an engagement with the debate about governmentality. This Report extends from consideration of the role of the Chief Constable down to what happens within every community. The Report thus introduces the governmentality debate to Northern Ireland and the Community Crime Survey provides an important resource in understanding the possible directions that this debate might take.

The Patten Report offers '*A New Beginning*'. Although it is subtitled '*Policing in Northern Ireland*', it is not about operational policing, but rather a report on the structures that should be implemented in order to allow for policing. The Report stresses that the police should be accountable within 'a real partnership between the police and the community - government agencies, non-governmental organisations, families, citizens; a partnership based on openness and understanding; a partnership in which policing reflects and responds to the community's needs' (Patten, 1999; Section 1:16). This involves, in the words of the Report, becoming 'more de-centralised; for the management style, which should become more open and delegated; and for the manner of policing down to beat level, which should become more orientated towards active problem-solving and crime prevention, rather than more traditional, reactive enforcement' (Patten, 1999, Section 1:16). The whole report is imbued with stressing the importance of human rights, community policing, partnership, neighbourhood and problem-solving. Management is to become more de-centralised with an increased emphasis on ideas of efficiency, effectiveness and accountability. The use of information technology and techniques of audit are strongly endorsed. Overall though, it affords the opportunity for a radical transformation of policing in Northern Ireland and more broadly how the problems of crime are perceived and indeed managed.

Since its establishment in 1922 the RUC has been identified with the interests of one community and one ideology at the expense of the other. It has been placed in the role of the defender of the state rather than the impartial protector of the law and civil order. Exigencies now have demanded that alternative approaches be adopted in the post-ceasefire circumstances. A neutral stance must now be formally and demonstrably assumed. This is to be based on problem solving and cost/benefit analysis in order to deal with the respective problems of crime and policing in the new society.

Such an approach allows the RUC to be proposed, not as a military style, hierarchical force, 'commanded rather than managed' (Patten, 1999, Section 10.2), but instead as a police service that aspires to enjoy acceptance and support in all of the communities in Northern Ireland. This entails the replacement of a sovereign force exercising government and control over tractable or recalcitrant subjects with a police service that works with willing and responsible communities and individuals *in their own governance*. Whether or not that can be achieved is a different matter, but what is important now is the way in which structures and networks are created for the exchange of information, and how power is devolved down with the words of command being replaced by the vocabulary of governmentality invoking partnership, flexibility, co-operation, problem solving, risk management and cost/benefit analysis.

This is a language of neutrality designed to afford the police service the same status as other services provided by government and local authorities such as the Housing Executive or the street cleaning services. It is intended to render crime an ordinary fact of everyday life. However, caution should be exercised in assumptions regarding the neutrality of policing. While some useful insights may be gleaned from a comparison of policing with other public and government services, one should remain mindful that policing entails, in the final analysis, a necessary component of coercive power. With that in mind, nonetheless the kinds of methods and strategies envisaged in the Patten report, begin to talk of policing *with* communities rather than policing *of* communities.

Such a view also recognises that crime cannot be eradicated. It can only be controlled and its effects mitigated. But this must involve not simply the police. Other agencies - governmental and non-governmental - and other groups down to individual communities and individual householders are now to be seen a part of the solution in this partnership approach.

Security and Control

The various issues that the Communities Crime Survey is concerned with centre primarily on the subject of security: both in the sense of being able to experience a feeling of safety and the means that are employed to attain that end. The question of security embraces the issues of how the different communities evaluate the security of their communities, their homes and their children with regard to a range of problems, but particularly those emanating from around crime, and the best manner in which security can be achieved and exercised. By addressing these issues from the perspectives of the various communities examined in the Survey we hope to both inform and reflect the debate about crime and policing in Northern Ireland.

Perhaps the central tenet of the Northern Ireland Communities Crime Survey has been to underline and acknowledge the 'lived' differences between the communities studied. Individuals' attitudes towards policing, crime, fear of crime and the range of issues explored in this study have been quite clearly conditioned by the nature of the communities in which they live. Our proposal, through the empirical findings of this Survey, is to offer a more informed account of the differing needs and experiences of the various communities within Northern Ireland. As Stenson puts it, 'the use of local surveys about victimisation and consumers' view of the service provided by the police, makes thinkable in calculable form a community diagnosis and a set of (hopefully) realisable objectives and priorities for crime prevention and control' (Stenson, 1993, p.381)[3].

---

[3] Indeed, it is interesting that the Patten Report itself quotes from the original report of the Communities Crime Survey as it was prepared for the Northern Ireland Office (Patten 1999: section 3.8).

As clearly evident in our study, the communities had stark physical, social and environmental differences. For example, in the urban lower working class areas, there were considerably higher levels of dissatisfaction with the environment concerning such issues as poor housing and inadequate amenities. Many in such communities saw unemployment as a major problem for their area. In the middle class areas, the physical environment was clearly much better and few regarded issues such as unemployment as problematic. Similarly working class communities experienced greater difficulties such as disturbances from teenagers, public drunkenness and neighbourhood disputes then their middle class or small town counterparts. Urban dwellers, both lower working class and middle class, had a different experience of crime, victimisation and fear of crime than those in the small town communities. Most obviously with regard to policing, the problematic relationship between the lower working class Catholic communities and the RUC and the involvement of paramilitaries in 'policing activities' in both lower working class Catholic and Protestant communities marked them apart from the other communities in the study. Also, with regard to both crime prevention and questions relating to children's safety and public space, there were considerable variances across the different community types. Thus, having underlined these differences, the imperative for institutions of the state and civil society is to find creative and *differing* modes of engaging with a range of community types.

For Foucault governmentality had 'as its essential technical means apparatuses of security' (1991, p.102). But those apparatuses of security could only be exercised with the freedom of the subject over whom power is being exercised: 'when one defines the exercises of power as a mode of action upon the actions of others, when one characterises these actions by the government of men by other men - in the broadest sense of the term - one includes an important element: freedom. Power is exercised only over free subjects, and only insofar as they are free' (Foucault, 1982, p.221). Thus, governmental action by itself cannot attain its own ends; it requires the willing co-operation of the individual subject participating in their own governance. Without this it is simply the imposition of the sovereign will on compliant or recalcitrant subjects. That dichotomy of compliance and recalcitrance has to a large extent characterised the debate on crime and policing amidst the 'two communities' of Northern Ireland. We argue that it is in fact more complex than this: there are indeed more than two communities and those different communities perceive the issues of crime and policing in a less reductionist manner than has often hitherto been appreciated.

Throughout this work we have sought to explore the attitudes and experiences of those different communities, and how they deal with the problems and fears evoked by crime and policing. We have sought to frame this within the context of governmentality which moves the debate about crime and policing beyond immediate political dimensions into discussions of the way that we live with each other. This is a debate about ethics, about the 'conduct of conduct'.

Foucault argued that: '...if you try to analyse power not on the basis of freedom, strategies, and governmentality, but on the basis of the political institution, you can only conceive of the subject as a subject of law. One then has a subject who has or does not have rights, who has had those rights either granted or removed by the institution of political society; and all this brings us back to a legal concept of the subject. On the other hand, I believe that the concept of governmentality makes it possible to bring out the freedom of the subject and its relationship to others - which constitute the very stuff [matière] of ethics' (1997, p.300).

This book has sought to explore fundamental aspects of how some communities live together, and in relation to the state, and to frame this in terms of a concept of governmentality. This exploration suggests complexity and provides a vivid illustration of the 'very stuff' of the challenges facing the new Northern Ireland.

Appendix 1: Survey Design and Methodology

The concept of 'community' is central to the whole analysis used in this survey. As discussed in chapters one and two, this survey aimed to look beyond the 'individual' as the unit of analysis, that is, beyond the individual's characteristics, such as their age, religion and sex. Rather, the survey focused on how communities and local circumstances impact upon the individual. The key reason for using the community as the basic unit of analysis was to explore the degree to which differing living environments, social conditions and the fabric of particular communities effects the experiences and attitudes of individuals in those communities.

Selection of the Communities

In selecting communities for this study, a number of factors that clearly differentiate communities from each other were identified (primarily from the previous literature, see chapters one and two). These included the large urban, as opposed to small town character of communities, the effects of social deprivation, and the extent of religious segregation within communities.

Along these three dimensions of socio-economic deprivation, religious division, and urbanisation, a number of community groupings were selected to represent extremes in these dimensions. This is important as the objective of the research was to identify the possible impact of these differences on individuals. Hence, the community groupings that were of interest included those that were socio-economically deprived versus those communities that were very affluent, those communities that were highly religiously segregated versus those that were integrated and finally those communities based in large urban areas versus those in small towns or rural communities.

To define the differing communities, therefore, three broad categories were selected:
(i) urban, lower working class areas which were religiously divided,
(ii) urban, middle class areas which were religiously integrated, and
(iii) small town areas which were religiously divided but were not particularly socio-economically disadvantaged.

Since these three groupings only represent fairly extreme examples of *some* of the major divisions between communities, they should not be seen together to represent all of the range of communities in Northern Ireland - this was not the intention of this survey. Rather they simply offer an insight in to just a few of the more dramatic divisions across communities in Northern Ireland.

Table A.1 shows the three major community groupings that were selected. As can be seen, from these major groupings a total of five differing *types* of communities were then selected:
(i) predominantly Catholic lower working class urban communities,
(ii) predominantly Protestant lower working class urban communities,
(iii) religiously mixed middle class urban areas,
(iv) the small town areas predominantly Catholic, and
(v) the small town areas predominantly Protestant.

Table A.1   Choice of Community Types Included in the Survey

A Urban, Lower Working Class Religiously Divided		B Urban Middle Class Mixed Religiously	C Small Town Middle Class Religiously Divided	
1 Catholic Lower Working Class Urban	2 Protestant Lower Working Class Urban	3 Mixed Religion Upper Middle Class Urban	4 Catholic Small Town	5 Protestant Small Town
4 Wards n=312	3 Wards n=290	3 Wards n=441	2 Wards n=286	2 Wards n=292

Criteria Used to Select the Communities

To select communities for inclusion in the survey a range of independent sources of information were employed. The electoral ward was used as the basic unit of analysis. The electoral ward was chosen for a number of reasons. Firstly, electoral wards are defined on the basis of being areas that contain similar housing and community conditions. In Northern Ireland they also correspond closely with clear community boundaries. This made them attractive for our purposes as we sought to explore community dimensions. Secondly, they are relatively small and contain around 3,000 individuals or about 1,000 households. They are also relatively small geographically, especially in the urban areas, and therefore, define easily identifiable communities. Lastly, electoral wards have also been commonly used as the basis of analysis in other research, particularly studies examining social and economic conditions and have been the subject of intense analysis on socio-economic deprivation in Northern Ireland (Robson *et al.*, 1994).

In order to ascertain religious division, the Northern Ireland Census (1991) was used. This provided a detailed religious breakdown of each ward in Northern Ireland and allowed communities to be chosen that were highly segregated in comparison to those that were religiously integrated. For the large urban versus small town or rural communities a geographical divide was used whereby the Belfast District Area was used in order to delineate the urban/small town divide. The small town areas and wards within them were then chosen individually so as to ensure they were outside the commuter belt of Belfast, they were similar to each other in terms of geographical size and housing density and they represented a good geographical spread across Northern Ireland.

The results of a comprehensive study of relative deprivation in Northern Ireland was employed to measure the socio-economic status of the communities, or their relative levels of economic deprivation. Amongst other things, this study placed all the wards in Northern Ireland in rank order according to their relative socio-economic deprivation (see Robson *et al.*, 1994) and allowed areas to be chosen that had high levels of socio economic deprivation versus areas of relative affluence.

Together these sources of information ensured that a range of independent and objective data could be used to select the communities for the survey.

For each of the five different community types (see Table A.1. above), a number of specific criteria were then used to select the wards which could be included in the survey. For the urban, lower working class and religiously divided communities; wards were chosen in the Belfast district area, which had at least a 90/10 per cent division according to religion and were in the bottom fifth of the matrix deprivation rank order (a rank score of below 110 for Northern Ireland). These wards were then considered in terms of their relative geographical positions in the Belfast area in order to ensure a good geographical spread of wards and thus avoid concentrating on just one part of the city.

For the urban, middle class, religiously mixed areas; wards from within the Belfast urban district area were chosen which had a matrix deprivation rank order in the top fifth for Northern Ireland (a rank order of 440 or above). The wards were also chosen to have no more than a 60/40 per cent divide according to religion using the Census data.

Lastly, for the small town divided communities; wards were chosen which were in small towns, outside the main commuter belt of Belfast and which gave a good geographical spread across Northern Ireland. The small town wards were also chosen to be of similar geographical size and housing density, to avoid picking very isolated communities dispersed across large ward areas. The wards were also selected to have at least an 80/20 per cent religious split according to Census data and to be in the in the mid-range of the relative deprivation rank order.

Using the criteria set out above, a number of wards were identified and selected to represent each of the five differing community types. The main reason for choosing a number of wards for each community type was to ensure that a number of different examples of the types of communities of interest were included and also to avoid picking individual areas which may have had particular characteristics or conditions that could have made them unrepresentative of that 'community type'. However, it must be said that, as with any type of sampling procedure used in surveys, there were limitations to the sampling process.

In many respects the use of 'community types' used in this survey is artificial, as there are differences within communities and differences in how a community could be defined. Further, like any other survey there is a certain degree to which the choice of areas from which the sample is drawn is somewhat subjective in nature. However, given the use of a range of independent and objective measures and the application of a strict selection criteria, there is reason for confidence that the selected samples chosen from the differing wards do represent distinctive community types.

Table A.2 outlines the number of wards selected in each of the community types and the number of interviews sought in each of the communities. As can be seen, the target was a total of 1,650 interviews, spread across the five differing community types.

Table A.2   Number of Wards and Interviews Selected for each of the Community Types

	Catholic Lower Working Class Urban	Protestant Lower Working Class Urban	Mixed Middle Class Urban	Catholic Small Towns	Protestant Small Towns
Number of wards selected	4	3	3	2	2
Number of interviews aimed for	300	300	450	300	300

Three wards were originally selected for the Catholic lower working class areas. However this was increased to four because of lower than expected response rates in these areas (see section on interviews and response rates).

Interviews and Response Rates

The main field work for the survey took place over a seven-week period from the 18th of March to the 2nd of April 1996. These dates are important for the survey because it took place shortly after the breakdown of the IRA cease-fire following the London Docklands bombing. The cease-fire had operated over a period of some sixteen months prior to this and during that time there had been a period of general public optimism. As such, the future prospects for Northern Ireland were considered to be brighter than they had been for some considerable time. However, the mood in Northern Ireland with respect to its future, at the time the interviews were conducted, was by no means as optimistic as it may have been in the period of the cease-fires, prior to the Docklands bombing.

The interviews were conducted by an experienced local survey company who had previously conducted many interviews in similar areas and had direct experience of working in areas that were very socio-economically disadvantaged and highly divided on religious grounds. All of the interviews took place on a face to face basis in the respondents' homes and the interviewers employed the computer assisted personal interviewer technique (C.A.P.I.), whereby notebook computers, rather than paper based questionnaires were used.

The interviews themselves lasted between 30 and 90 minutes, with the longer interviews being with those that had a number of victimisation incidents to report and those with larger households (where information on children was gathered).

The households chosen for interview were selected at random from the postal address file. In each household a respondent over the age of sixteen was selected at random using the Kish Grid method and the interviewers were not allowed to take substitutes. The selection process aimed to provide a random selection of individuals of sixteen years of age or older within the five main community types (as in Table A2).

In line with normal practice, the data obtained from the survey process were later adjusted or 'weighted' to correct for the under-representation of individuals living in households with more than one adult. This is because the chance of an adult being selected for interview is inversely related to the number of adults in the household. The weighted data are used when reference is made to individuals, such as for 'assault' or 'theft from the person', while unweighted data are used in relation to household incidents like 'burglary' or 'thefts from outside the home'.

As noted above, the aim was to obtain a total of 1,650 completed interviews across the differing community types. Each household selected for inclusion was initially sent an introductory letter explaining the nature of the survey, its importance and requesting their co-operation. An interviewer then called at the selected address and attempted to complete the interview with a specific respondent using the Kish Grid selection process. Up to five call backs were made per-address, if necessary, to obtain the interview with the selected respondent and no substitutes were permitted.

A total of 2,839 addresses were selected for possible inclusion in this survey. Some 5.8 per cent of the addresses were not eligible for inclusion in the survey by reason of being vacant or demolished (see Table A.3 for details of response rates). This left an eligible sample of 2,683 households. Some 21.8 per cent of the eligible households refused to partake in the interview - by either contacting us after they had received the introductory letter or by declining to be interviewed when they were approached by an interviewer. A debriefing with the interviewers and contacts with possible respondents revealed that the vast majority of refusals were made on the grounds that the respondents did not have the time available to be interviewed, rather than any objections to the nature of the questionnaire. A further 17.7 per cent of the eligible interviewees were not available for interview despite up to five calls being made to their address. This left an overall completion rate of 60.4 per cent of the eligible addresses.

The achieved completion rate of 60.4 per cent is lower than some recent national surveys (e.g. The 1992 British Crime Survey completion rate was 77 per cent). However, this rate is similar to some other local crime surveys (e.g. the 1990 Edinburgh Crime Survey, completion rate 62.3 per cent) and is actually better than some community based crime surveys which concentrated on areas with high levels of socio-economic deprivation (e.g. The Dundee Safer Cities Project Surveys 1991 and 1994, completion rate 40 per cent and 42 per cent respectively).

It is noteworthy that some of the lowest completion rates were in areas with the greatest socio-economic deprivation. This is similar to the experiences of the Dundee surveys (1993, 1995) which were conducted in a number of lower working class council estates and also had a high proportion of refusals. Completion rates, in this survey, were especially low in the Catholic lower working class communities (see Table A.3 below).

In one of the lower working class Catholic wards the interviews were called off because the interviewers felt threatened and uncomfortable in the area. An interviewer was told by a group of people in a house in this ward that he was not welcome in the area. While it was not clear that this was an organised attempt at intimidation by paramilitaries or any other grouping, the decision was taken by the research management committee not to place any field workers in a ward where they felt less than comfortable. A substitute ward was picked using exactly the same selection criteria and the interviews continued in the substitute ward.

Table A.3   Completion Rates by Community Types

	Catholic Lower Working Class Urban	Protestant Lower Working Class Urban	Mixed Middle Class Urban	Catholic Small Towns	Protestant Small Towns
Total sample selected for inclusion	737	476	742	437	447
Vacant / Demolished or empty properties	63	29	20	20	24
Viable sample	674	447	722	417	423
Five calls	155	77	137	54	54
Refusal	208	80	144	77	77
Completed interviews	312	290	441	286	292
Per cent completed	46	65	61	69	69

Overall Completion Rates

Total Sample Selected	2839
Vacant/Demolished Empty	156
Viable	2683
5 Calls	476 (17.7%)
Refused	586 (21.8%)
Completed	1621 (60.4%)

An important implication of the generally lower completion rates found in areas which were socio-economically deprived is that surveys in general and national cross-sectional surveys specifically, may under-represent individuals from such areas. This survey shows that completion rates were especially low for the Catholic lower working class communities. Surveys conducted in Northern Ireland should therefore pay particular attention this issue in order to ensure that such populations are adequately represented in their sample. One of the advantages of this survey is that such communities were targeted for inclusion and this enabled the identification of such differences in completion rates.

Representativeness of the Sample

A number of factors relating to the sample included in the survey were examined in order to determine how well the sample matched the populations residing in the various communities. Firstly, in relation to the levels of socio-economic deprivation - Table A.4 outlines the average deprivation rank score for each of the community types. As can be seen, there are very clear differences between the communities. Both of the lower working class community types (Catholic and Protestant) have average deprivation scores well below the bottom fifth of the matrix deprivation rank order (rank score of 110) - in fact these areas were among some of the most socio-economically deprived areas in Northern Ireland. They are also, on average, very different from the other community types selected for inclusion in the survey (see Table A.4 below).

With regard to religious division, it was possible to compare the 1991 Census data for each of the wards selected from the differing community types with the responses obtained in those communities. The aim was to obtain a very religiously divided sample in the lower working class communities, a more religiously integrated sample in the middle class communities and a divided sample in the small town areas. As can be seen in Table A.5, the sample matched very closely with the census data and the divisions according to religion were clearly evident between the different community types.

The 1991 census data from the differing communities according to sex and age categories were also compared with the sample interviewed (See Tables A.6 and A.7). With respect to sex, it can be seen that the sample closely approximated the distribution of men and women in the communities as found in the 1991 census data (see Table A.6 below). With respect to the distribution across age categories, it also appears that the survey was able to obtain a well distributed sample, closely matching the census data for 1991.

Overall, by comparing the sample with other independent sources such as Census data, it is evident that the sample obtained was closely representative of the populations residing in the wards which made up our community types.

Table A.4 Average Deprivation Rank Order Scores for Community Types

	Catholic Lower Working Class Urban	Protestant Lower Working Class Urban	Mixed Middle Class Urban	Catholic Small Towns	Protestant Small Towns
Average deprivation rank order score	26	46	508	297	293

Table A.5 Religious Division by Community Types (per cent): 1991 Census Data and Survey Respondents

	Catholic Lower Working Class Urban	Protestant Lower Working Class Urban	Mixed Middle Class Urban	Catholic Small Towns	Protestant Small Towns
1991 Census data					
Protestant	3	96	53	15	85
Catholic	96	4	46	86	14
Sample surveyed					
Protestant	0.6	89.3	45.7	6.5	75.3
Catholic	96.5	7.5	49.4	89.8	19.2
None/Other	3	3.1	4.8	3.7	5.4

Table A.6 Sex by Community Type (per cent): 1991 Census Data and Survey Respondents

	Catholic Lower Working Class Urban	Protestant Lower Working Class Urban	Mixed Middle Class Urban	Catholic Small Towns	Protestant Small Towns
1991 Census data					
Male	47	46	46	49	47
Female	53	54	54	51	53
Sample surveyed					
Male	53	48	48	53	52
Female	47	52	52	47	48

Table A.7 Age by Community Type (per cent): 1991 Census Data and Survey Respondents

	Catholic Lower Working Class Urban	Protestant Lower Working Class Urban	Mixed Middle Class Urban	Catholic Small Towns	Protestant Small Towns
1991 Census data					
16-24	22	16	16	23	17
25-34	22	19	20	21	53
35-44	14	12	17	18	16
45-54	13	15	13	13	15
55-64	14	14	12	10	13
65+	16	25	23	18	23
Sample surveyed					
16-24	18	15	18	20	14
25-34	19	15	17	21	13
35-44	22	16	18	18	20
45-54	14	18	21	20	23

Appendix 2: The Questionnaire[1]

Introduction
How long have you lived in this <u>house</u>?
Less than 1 year ☐   1-3 years ☐   3+years ☐
All of your life ☐

How long have you lived in this <u>area</u> (i.e. within an easy walk of your home)? [*This definition is used for all questions that refer to this particular 'area'*]
Less than 1 year ☐   1-3 years ☐   3+years ☐
All of your life ☐

(If moved area in last 3 years)
Were any of these reasons relevant for moving to this area?

	RELEVANT	NOT RELEVANT
You liked the area	☐	☐
You were near family (or partner's)	☐	☐
You were brought up here (or partner)	☐	☐
Cost of housing	☐	☐
Safety from sectarian attack	☐	☐
Availability of housing	☐	☐
Safety from crime	☐	☐
Near shops / amenities	☐	☐
Near work (or partner's)	☐	☐

Were there any other relevant reasons for moving to this area?
.... (please specify)

---

[1] This questionnaire was administered using the Computer Assisted Personal Interview (CAPI) technique, by which face to face interviews were conducted using note book computers rather than paper based questionnaires.

Overall, how satisfied are you with living in this area?
Very satisfied ☐
Fairly satisfied ☐
Fairly dissatisfied ☐
Very dissatisfied ☐
No opinion ☐

How would you feel about moving away from this area? Would you be:
Very pleased ☐
Fairly pleased ☐
A bit sorry ☐
Very sorry ☐
Would you have mixed feelings? ☐
No opinion ☐

Would you like to move from this area?   Yes ☐   No ☐
If you would like to move, please give the main reason why.

In general, what kind of neighbourhood would you say you live in?
Would you say it is a neighbourhood in which people do things together and try to help each other, or one in which people mostly go their own way?
Help each other ☐
Go own way ☐
Mixture ☐
DK/NA ☐

I'd like to <u>show you a card</u> of things that people often complain about. Could you tell me how much of a problem this is in your area <u>at present</u>?
Big problem=1   Bit of a problem=2   No Real Problem=3   Don't Know=4

	1	2	3	4
1. Poor street lighting	☐	☐	☐	☐
2. Poor housing	☐	☐	☐	☐
3. Drug abuse (including dealing)	☐	☐	☐	☐
4. Sectarian harassment	☐	☐	☐	☐

5. Racial harassment □ □ □ □
6. Paramilitary harassment □ □ □ □
7. Police harassment □ □ □ □
8. Unemployment □ □ □ □
9. Empty properties □ □ □ □
10. Poor public transport □ □ □ □
11. Violence in the home □ □ □ □
12. Litter and graffiti □ □ □ □
13. Vandalism □ □ □ □
14. Arson □ □ □ □
15. Nuisance from noise □ □ □ □
16. Poor shopping facilities □ □ □ □
17. Little for teenagers to do □ □ □ □
18. Public drunkenness □ □ □ □
19. Uncontrolled dogs □ □ □ □
20. Disturbances from teenagers □ □ □ □
21. Poor parental control □ □ □ □
22. Under-age drinking □ □ □ □
23. Not safe for children □ □ □ □
24. Parades and demonstrations □ □ □ □
25. Vehicle theft □ □ □ □
26. Neighbourhood disputes □ □ □ □
27. Joy riding □ □ □ □
28. Punishment beatings □ □ □ □

You have identified the following problems in the area. (S*how list*)
What do you consider to be the biggest or most pressing problem <u>in this area</u>? ---

AFTER COMPLETION OF LIST, AND ONLY FOR THOSE WHO HAVE LIVED IN THE AREA FOR AT LEAST 3 YEARS, FILL IN SECTION ON CHANGE DURING THE CEASE-FIRES.

(*Interviewer; show card and enter only those items that have changed.*)
In general, do you think any of these problems changed (ie. got better or worse) <u>during the period of the cease-fires</u>? [Cease-fires: from October 1994 to February 1996 when both sides were operating cease-fires] (*Show Card*)

Better now	1	About same	2
Worse	3	Don't know	4

	1	2	3	4
1. Poor street lighting	☐	☐	☐	☐
2. Poor housing	☐	☐	☐	☐
3. Drug abuse (including dealing)	☐	☐	☐	☐
4. Sectarian harassment	☐	☐	☐	☐
5. Racial harassment	☐	☐	☐	☐
6. Paramilitary harassment	☐	☐	☐	☐
7. Police harassment	☐	☐	☐	☐
8. Unemployment	☐	☐	☐	☐
9. Empty properties	☐	☐	☐	☐
10. Poor public transport	☐	☐	☐	☐
11. Violence in the home	☐	☐	☐	☐
12. Litter and graffiti	☐	☐	☐	☐
13. Vandalism	☐	☐	☐	☐
14. Arson	☐	☐	☐	☐
15. Nuisance from noise	☐	☐	☐	☐
16. Poor shopping facilities	☐	☐	☐	☐
17. Little for teenagers to do	☐	☐	☐	☐
18. Public drunkenness	☐	☐	☐	☐
19. Uncontrolled dogs	☐	☐	☐	☐
20. Disturbances from teenagers	☐	☐	☐	☐
21. Poor parental control	☐	☐	☐	☐
22. Under-age drinking	☐	☐	☐	☐
23. Not safe for children	☐	☐	☐	☐
24. Parades and demonstrations	☐	☐	☐	☐
25. Vehicle theft	☐	☐	☐	☐
26. Neighbourhood disputes	☐	☐	☐	☐
27. Joy riding	☐	☐	☐	☐
28. Punishment beatings	☐	☐	☐	☐

Outside the neighbourhood:
I'd now like to ask you some questions relating to areas outside your neighbourhood <u>at present</u>. [Grid used for these questions]
Do you use ...
   (a)   Belfast city centre shopping   yes☐ no☐
   (b)   Belfast downtown cinemas   yes☐ no☐

(c)   Belfast downtown restaurants or pubs   yes☐   no ☐
(d)   Leisure/sports facilities outside neighbourhood yes☐ no☐

Is your personal safety a factor influencing your use of
(a)   Belfast city centre shopping   yes ☐ no ☐ NA ☐ Don't know☐
(b)   Belfast downtown cinemas   yes ☐ no ☐ NA ☐ Don't know☐
(c) Belfast downtown restaurants/pubs yes☐ no ☐ NA ☐ Don't know☐
(d) Leisure/sports facilities outside your neighbourhood yes ☐ no ☐ NA ☐ Don't know☐

If yes to any, ask as appropriate.
How often in the <u>average</u> month would you visit ?
1=daily, 2=more than once a week, 3=weekly, 4=fortnightly, 5=monthly,
6=less than 1 per month, 7=only special occasions, 9=don't know.
(a)   Belfast city centre shopping ....
(b)   Belfast downtown cinema.................
(c)   Belfast downtown restaurants or pubs...................
(d)   Leisure/sports facilities outside your neighbourhood ....

How safe do you feel using ....
very safe=1   fairly safe=2   neither safe nor unsafe=3   fairly unsafe=4
very unsafe=5
(a)   Belfast city centre shopping   1 2 3 4 5
(b)   Belfast downtown cinemas   1 2 3 4 5
(c)   Belfast downtown restaurants or pubs   1 2 3 4 5
(d)   Leisure/sports facilities outside neighbourhood   1 2 3 4 5

In general, did your use of ... increase during the period of the cease-fires?
(a)   Belfast city centre shopping   yes☐   no ☐
(b)   Belfast downtown cinemas   yes☐   no ☐
(c)   Belfast downtown restaurants or pubs   yes☐   no ☐
(d)   Leisure/sports facilities outside neighbourhood yes☐ no☐

SAFETY and CRIME in this area
I would now like to ask you some questions about crime and your safety <u>in this area</u>. Firstly, we will now give you a number of hypothetical situations and ask how you would respond in each case.

Please rank 1-3 in terms of your most likely action
[If respondent answers 'it depends', stress that question seeks to find out what you <u>might</u> do without being specific about details. *Don't Prompt, looking for qualitative information*]

(a) Young people frequently making noise late at night outside your house. What would you do?..
Please specify, (eg. call the police, deal with it yourself, inform a resident's association or community group, talk to neighbours, etc.)

(b) Witness a property crime such as someone breaking a neighbour's window?   [*Don't Prompt*]
What would you do?..
Please specify, (eg. call the police, deal with it yourself, inform a resident's association or community group, talk to neighbours, etc.)

(c) Witness a property crime such as burglary in this area?
[*Don't Prompt*]
What would you do?..
Please specify, (eg. call the police, deal with it yourself, inform a resident's association, or community group talk to neighbours, etc.)

(d) You suspect that someone in your neighbourhood physically abuses their children?   [*Don't Prompt*]
What would you do?..
Please specify, (eg. call the police, deal with it yourself, do nothing, inform a resident's association, community group, talk to neighbours, etc.)

(e) If you were hit, punched or kicked by someone in the street?
[*Don't Prompt*]
What would you do?..
Please specify, (eg. call the police, deal with it yourself, do nothing, inform a resident's association, community group, talk to neighbours, etc.)

Whenever you are alone in your home at night, do you feel:
Very safe? ☐ Safe? ☐ A bit unsafe? ☐ Very unsafe? ☐ Don't know? ☐

How much do you worry about having your home broken into?

Very worried? ☐ Fairly worried? ☐ Not very worried? ☐
Not at all worried ☐

For this house, or any other house in which you have lived <u>in this area</u> (i.e....), has anyone ever got in without permission <u>and stolen anything or caused damage inside the house</u>?
Yes ☐   No ☐   **IF NO, GO TO NEXT**

How many times in last 12 months?
1 ☐ 2 ☐ 3 ☐ 4 ☐ 5 ☐ 5+ ☐

On the last occasion, did it occur:
During the day? ☐   After dark? ☐

On the last occasion, were the police informed?
Yes ☐   No ☐   DK/NA ☐

Did you seek help from:	Yes	No
Friends / Relatives	☐	☐
Local Community Group	☐	☐
General Practitioner	☐	☐
Clergy (Priest/ Minister)	☐	☐
Other Individual and/or Organisation (Specify) _____	☐	☐
None of the above	☐	☐

If yes, how helpful did you find them to be?
[*Use categories:*   *Very helpful, Helpful, Not helpful at all, DK*]

Friends / Relatives	☐	☐	☐	☐
Local Community Group	☐	☐	☐	☐
General Practitioner	☐	☐	☐	☐
Clergy (Priest/ Minister)	☐	☐	☐	☐
Other Individual and/or	☐	☐	☐	☐

Organisation (Specify)
_____

Sometimes, things that people are carrying are stolen - from their hand, pocket or bag.
Is this something you worry about <u>in this area</u>?
Very worried ☐   Fairly worried ☐   Not very worried ☐
Not at all worried ☐

Has anything like that ever happened to you? (*Specify most recent*)
....
....

IF NO, GO TO NEXT, IF YES, how many times in the last 12 months?
(<u>anywhere</u>)   0 ☐   1 ☐   2 ☐
              3 ☐   4 ☐   5+ ☐

How many times in the last 12 months <u>in this area</u>?
0 ☐   1 ☐   2 ☐   3 ☐
4 ☐   5+ ☐

On the last occasion, were the police informed?
Yes ☐   No ☐   Don't know/NA ☐

Did you seek help from:	Yes	No
Friends / Relatives	☐	☐
Local Community Group	☐	☐
General Practitioner	☐	☐
Clergy (Priest/ Minister)	☐	☐
Other Individual and/or Organisation (Specify)	☐	☐

_____
None of the above   ☐   ☐

If yes, how helpful did you find them to be?
[*Use categories: Very helpful, Helpful, Not helpful at all, DK*]
Friends / Relatives   ☐   ☐   ☐   ☐

Local Community Group	☐	☐	☐	☐
General Practitioner	☐	☐	☐	☐
Clergy (Priest/ Minister)	☐	☐	☐	☐
Other Individual and/or Organisation (Specify)	☐	☐	☐	☐

_____

Sometimes people are assaulted or attacked - by fists, by kicks or by weapons. **(TO WOMEN:** I'm excluding for the moment sexual attacks).Is this something you worry about?
Very worried? ☐ Fairly worried? ☐ Not very worried? ☐
Not at all worried? ☐

Has anything like that ever happened to you? (Specify most recent)
....

IF NO, GO TO NEXT, IF YES, How many times in the last 12 months? (anywhere)
0 ☐ 1 ☐ 2 ☐ 3 ☐
4 ☐ 5+ ☐

IF YES, how many times in last 12 months in this area?
0 ☐ 1 ☐ 2 ☐ 3 ☐
4 ☐ 5+ ☐

On the last occasion, were the police informed?
Yes ☐   No ☐   DK/NA ☐

Did you seek help from: Yes   No
Friends / Relatives   ☐   ☐
Local Community Group   ☐   ☐
General Practitioner   ☐   ☐
Clergy (Priest/ Minister)   ☐   ☐

Other Individual and/or   ☐   ☐

Organisation (Specify)
_____

None of the above ☐ ☐

If yes, how helpful did you find them to be?
[*Use categories: Very helpful, Helpful, Not helpful at all, DK*]

Friends / Relatives ☐ ☐ ☐ ☐
Local Community Group ☐ ☐ ☐ ☐
General Practitioner ☐ ☐ ☐ ☐
Clergy (Priest/Minister) ☐ ☐ ☐ ☐
Other Individual and/or Organisation (Specify) ☐ ☐ ☐ ☐

_____

People are sometimes <u>harassed, frightened or upset</u> by strangers staring, following them on foot or by car, pestering them or whatever (eg. stalking).

Is this something you worry about <u>in this area</u>?
Very worried? ☐ Fairly worried? ☐ Not very worried? ☐   Not at all worried? ☐

Has anything like that ever happened to you? (Specify most recent, eg. followed by man, or pestered by stranger.)
....
....

IF NO, GO TO NEXT,   **IF YES,** How many times in the last 12 months? (<u>anywhere</u>)
0 ☐   1 ☐   2 ☐   3 ☐
4 ☐   5+ ☐

How many times in the last 12 months <u>in this area</u>?
0 ☐   1 ☐   2 ☐   3 ☐
4 ☐   5+ ☐

On the last occasion, were the police informed?
Yes ☐   No ☐   Don't know/NA ☐

Did you seek help from:	Yes	No
Friends / Relatives	☐	☐
Local Community Group	☐	☐
General Practitioner	☐	☐
Clergy (Priest/Minister)	☐	☐
Other Individual and/or Organisation (Specify) _____	☐	☐
None of the above	☐	☐

If yes, how helpful did you find them to be?
   [*Use categories: Very helpful, Helpful, Not helpful at all, DK*]

Friends / Relatives	☐	☐	☐	☐
Local Community Group	☐	☐	☐	☐
General Practitioner	☐	☐	☐	☐
Clergy (Priest/Minister)	☐	☐	☐	☐
Other Individual and/or Organisation (Specify) _____	☐	☐	☐	☐

Sometimes people or their families are **threatened** with violence or with damage to their property (excluding threats from the person(s) you live with, i.e. domestic violence). Is this something you worry about?
Very worried? ☐ Fairly worried? ☐   Not very worried? ☐   Not at all worried? ☐

Has anything like that ever happened to you? (Specify most recent)
....

IF NO GO TO NEXT, IF YES,
How many times in the last 12 months? (<u>anywhere</u>)
0   ☐   1   ☐   2   ☐   3   ☐
4   ☐   5+   ☐

How many times in last 12 months <u>in this area</u>?
0 ☐   1 ☐   2 ☐   3 ☐
4 ☐   5+ ☐

On the last occasion, were the police informed?
Yes ☐   No ☐   DK/NA ☐

Did you seek help from:	Yes	No
Friends / Relatives	☐	☐
Local Community Group	☐	☐
General Practitioner	☐	☐
Clergy (Priest/Minister)	☐	☐
Other Individual and/or Organisation (Specify)	☐	☐
_____		
None of the above	☐	☐

If yes, how helpful did you find them to be?
[*Use categories: Very helpful, Helpful, Not helpful at all, DK*]

Friends / Relatives	☐	☐	☐	☐
Local Community Group	☐	☐	☐	☐
General Practitioner	☐	☐	☐	☐
Clergy (Priest/Minister)	☐	☐	☐	☐
Other Individual and/or Organisation (Specify)	☐	☐	☐	☐

_____

WOMEN ONLY
Sexual assaults on women by strangers do sometimes occur.

Is this something you worry about?
Very worried? ☐   Fairly worried? ☐   Not very worried? ☐
Not at all worried? ☐

Has this ever happened to you? yes ☐ no ☐

IF NO GO TO NEXT **IF YES,** How many times in the last 12 months? (anywhere)
0 ☐ 1 ☐ 2 ☐ 3 ☐
4 ☐ 5+ ☐

IF YES, how many times in last 12 months <u>in this area</u>?
0 ☐ 1 ☐ 2 ☐ 3 ☐
4 ☐ 5+ ☐

On the last occasion, were the police informed?
Yes ☐ No ☐ DK/NA ☐

Did you seek help from:	Yes	No
Friends / Relatives	☐	☐
Local Community Group	☐	☐
General Practitioner	☐	☐
Clergy (Priest/ Minister)	☐	☐
Other Individual and/or Organisation (Specify) _____	☐	☐
None of the above	☐	☐

If yes, how helpful did you find them to be?
[*Use categories:*   *Very helpful, Helpful, Not helpful at all, DK*]

Friends / Relatives	☐	☐	☐	☐
Local Community Group	☐	☐	☐	☐
General Practitioner	☐	☐	☐	☐
Clergy (Priest/ Minister)	☐	☐	☐	☐
Other Individual and/or Organisation (Specify) _____	☐	☐	☐	☐

ALL RESPONDENTS, SECTARIAN INCIDENTS

How worried are you about being subject to <u>verbal abuse</u> because of your religion?
Very worried? ☐ Fairly worried? ☐ Not very worried? ☐
Not at all worried? ☐

Has this ever happened to you?   Yes ☐   No ☐
[If 'yes' only]
How many times in the last 12 months <u>anywhere</u>? _____
How many times in the last 12 months in this <u>area</u> _____
Were the Police informed?   Yes ☐   No ☐

How worried are you about being subject to a physical attack because of your religion?
Very worried? ☐   Fairly worried? ☐   Not very worried? ☐
Not at all worried? ☐

Has this ever happened to you?   Yes ☐   No ☐
[If 'yes' only]

How many times in the last 12 months <u>anywhere</u>? _____

How many times in the last 12 months in this <u>area</u> _____

On the last occasion were the police informed?   Yes ☐ No ☐

How worried are you about your home being damaged because of your religion?
Very worried? ☐ Fairly worried? ☐ Not very worried? ☐
Not at all worried? ☐

Has this ever happened to you?   Yes ☐   No ☐
[If 'yes' only]

How many times in the last 12 months <u>anywhere</u>? _____

How many times in the last 12 months in this <u>area</u> _____

Appendix 2   157

On the last occasion were the police informed? Yes ☐ No ☐

How worried are you about being threatened because of your religion?
Very worried? ☐ Fairly worried? ☐ Not very worried? ☐
Not at all worried? ☐

Has this ever happened to you? Yes ☐ No ☐
[If 'yes' only]

How many times in the last 12 months <u>anywhere</u>? _____

How many times in the last 12 months in this <u>area</u> _____

On the last occasion were the police informed? Yes ☐ No ☐

How worried are you of being the victim of a bomb or other terrorist / paramilitary attack?
Very worried? ☐   Fairly worried? ☐   Not very worried? ☐
Not at all worried? ☐

Has this ever happened to you? Yes ☐   No ☐
[If 'yes' only]

How many times in the last 12 months <u>anywhere</u>? _____

How many times in the last 12 months in this <u>area</u> _____

On the last occasion were the police informed? Yes ☐ No ☐

Thinking about this area, how safe from ordinary crime do you feel walking alone around here?   ('Ordinary' crime is non-sectarian crime)

During the day		**After Dark**	
Very safe	☐	Very safe	☐
Safe	☐	Safe	☐
A bit unsafe	☐	A bit unsafe	☐
Very unsafe	☐	Very unsafe	☐
Don't know	☐	Don't know	☐

Purely as a precaution against ordinary crime around here, how often do you?

OFTEN=1   SOMETIMES=2   RARELY=3   NEVER=4

	DAYTIME [then ask]	AFTER DARK
	1 2 3 4	1 2 3 4
Avoid going out	☐ ☐ ☐ ☐	☐ ☐ ☐ ☐
Go out with someone rather than alone	☐ ☐ ☐ ☐	☐ ☐ ☐ ☐
Keep away from certain areas around here	☐ ☐ ☐ ☐	☐ ☐ ☐ ☐
Take a taxi rather than a bus or train	☐ ☐ ☐ ☐	☐ ☐ ☐ ☐
Carry some form of SelfDefence	☐ ☐ ☐ ☐	☐ ☐ ☐ ☐
Take a dog when you go out	☐ ☐ ☐ ☐	☐ ☐ ☐ ☐

(If no dog, ignore rest of dog questions)

FOR THOSE WHO HAVE LIVED IN AREA FOR 3 YEARS+ I would now like to ask you about any incidents you may have <u>seen</u> over the past 3 years <u>in this area</u>.

	Have you seen anybody?		Did you report it to the police?	
	YES	NO	YES	NO
Setting fire to property	☐	☐	☐	☐
Vandalising property	☐	☐	☐	☐
Breaking into a house	☐	☐	☐	☐
Shoplifting	☐	☐	☐	☐
Stealing from a vehicle	☐	☐	☐	☐
Stealing anything else	☐	☐	☐	☐
Selling, buying or using illegal drugs	☐	☐	☐	☐

Appendix 2   159

'Joy riding'
☐   ☐   ☐   ☐
In a serious fight
☐   ☐   ☐   ☐
Flashing (indecent exposure)
☐   ☐   ☐   ☐

Compared to the rest of Northern Ireland how much ordinary crime would you say there is in this area?   Would you say there is:
a lot more?   ☐
a little more?   ☐
about the same?   ☐
a little less?   ☐
a lot less?   ☐
DK/NA   ☐

Compared to Britain how much ordinary crime would you say there is in Northern Ireland?   Would you say there is:
a lot more?   ☐
a little more?   ☐
about the same?   ☐
a little less?   ☐
a lot less?   ☐
DK/NA   ☐

Compared to the Republic Ireland how much ordinary crime would you say there is in Northern Ireland?   Would you say there is:
a lot more?   ☐
a little more?   ☐
about the same?   ☐
a little less?   ☐
a lot less?   ☐
DK/NA   ☐

How much would you say the crime rate (ordinary) <u>here (this area)</u> changed during the cease fires?
a lot more   ☐
a little more?   ☐

about the same? ☐
a little less? ☐
a lot less? ☐
DK/NA ☐

In <u>Northern Ireland</u> would you say the crime rate (ordinary) changed during the period of the cease fires?
a lot more crime? ☐
a little more? ☐
about the same? ☐
a little less crime? ☐
a lot less? ☐
DK/NA ☐

I'd now like to ask you some questions about crime and safety affecting your home and belongings.   Let's start with bicycles, cars and motorbikes.
During the last 12 months, have you or anyone in this household owned or had personal use of a   bicycle   Yes ☐   No ☐
IF NO, GO TO NEXT

How much do you worry about the bike being stolen?
A lot ☐   Sometimes ☐   Rarely ☐   Never ☐

Has a bicycle belonging to your household ever been stolen?   Yes ☐   No ☐
IF NO GO TO NEXT

How many times in last 12 months? (<u>anywhere</u>)
0 ☐   1 ☐   2 ☐   3 ☐
4 ☐   5+ ☐

How many times in last 12 months in this area?
0 ☐   1 ☐   2 ☐   3 ☐
4 ☐   5+ ☐

On the last occasion, were the police informed?
Yes ☐   No ☐   Don't know/NA ☐

Did you seek help from:	Yes	No
Friends / Relatives	☐	☐
Local Community Group	☐	☐
General Practitioner	☐	☐
Clergy (Priest/ Minister)	☐	☐
Other Individual and/or Organisation (Specify) _____	☐	☐
None of the above	☐	☐

If yes, how helpful did you find them to be?
   [*Use categories: Very helpful, Helpful, Not helpful at all, DK*]

Friends / Relatives	☐	☐	☐	☐
Local Community Group	☐	☐	☐	☐
General Practitioner	☐	☐	☐	☐
Clergy (Priest/ Minister)	☐	☐	☐	☐
Other Individual and/or Organisation (Specify) _____	☐	☐	☐	☐

During the last 12 months, has anyone in your household owned or had personal use of: *motorbike* Yes ☐ No ☐
car Yes ☐ No ☐ *van* Yes ☐ No ☐
IF NO, TO NEXT

Where is (was) the vehicle parked overnight?   Garage ☐
Street ☐   Drive/Garden/Carport ☐

How much have you worried about the vehicle(s) being stolen?
A lot ☐   Quite a lot ☐   A Little ☐   Not at all ☐

Has a motor vehicle belonging to your household ever been stolen?
Yes ☐   No ☐   **IF NO, GO TO NEXT**

How many times in last 12 months? (<u>anywhere</u>)
0 ☐   1 ☐   2 ☐   3 ☐
4 ☐   5+ ☐

How many times in last 12 months in this ....area?
0 ☐   1 ☐   2 ☐   3 ☐
4 ☐   5+ ☐

On the last occasion, were the police informed?
Yes ☐   No ☐   Don't know/NA ☐

Did you seek help from:	Yes	No
Friends / Relatives	☐	☐
Local Community Group	☐	☐
General Practitioner	☐	☐
Clergy (Priest/Minister)	☐	☐
Other Individual and/or Organisation (Specify) _____	☐	☐
None of the above	☐	☐

If yes, how helpful did you find them to be?
[*Use categories: Very helpful, Helpful, Not helpful at all, DK*]

Friends / Relatives	☐	☐	☐	☐
Local Community Group	☐	☐	☐	☐
General Practitioner	☐	☐	☐	☐
Clergy (Priest/Minister)	☐	☐	☐	☐
Other Individual and/or Organisation (Specify)	☐	☐	☐	☐

How much have you worried about the vehicle having things stolen from it - parts of the vehicle, or the contents inside?
Very worried? ☐   Fairly worried? ☐   Not very worried? ☐
Not at all worried ☐

Has anything ever been stolen from any vehicle belonging to your household?
Yes ☐   No ☐   **IF NO, GO TO NEXT**

How many times in last 12 months? (<u>anywhere</u>)
0 ☐   1 ☐   2 ☐   3 ☐
4 ☐   5+ ☐

How many times in last 12 months in this ....area?
0 ☐   1 ☐   2 ☐   3 ☐
4 ☐   5+ ☐

On the last occasion, were the police informed?
Yes ☐   No ☐   Don't know/NA ☐

Did you seek help from:	Yes	No
Friends / Relatives	☐	☐
Local Community Group	☐	☐
General Practitioner	☐	☐
Clergy (Priest/Minister)	☐	☐
Other Individual and/or Organisation (Specify) _____	☐	☐
None of the above	☐	☐

If yes, how helpful did you find them to be?
   [*Use categories: Very helpful, Helpful, Not helpful at all, DK*]

Friends / Relatives	☐	☐	☐	☐
Local Community Group	☐	☐	☐	☐
General Practitioner	☐	☐	☐	☐
Clergy (Priest/Minister)	☐	☐	☐	☐
Other Individual and/or Organisation (Specify)	☐	☐	☐	☐

How much have you worried about the vehicle being vandalised?
Very worried? ☐ Fairly worried? ☐ Not very worried? ☐
Not at all worried? ☐

Has a vehicle belonging to your household ever been vandalised?
Yes ☐   No ☐   **IF NO, GO TO NEXT**

How many times in last 12 months? (<u>anywhere</u>)
0 ☐   1 ☐   2 ☐   3 ☐
4 ☐   5+ ☐

How many times in last 12 months in this ....area?
0 ☐   1 ☐   2 ☐   3 ☐
4 ☐   5+ ☐

On the last occasion, were the police informed?
Yes ☐   No ☐   Don't know/NA ☐

Did you seek help from:	Yes	No
Friends / Relatives	☐	☐
Local Community Group	☐	☐
General Practitioner	☐	☐
Clergy (Priest/Minister)	☐	☐
Other Individual and/or Organisation (Specify)	☐	☐
_____		
None of the above	☐	☐

If yes, how helpful did you find them to be?
  [*Use categories: Very helpful, Helpful, Not helpful at all, DK*]

Friends / Relatives	☐	☐	☐	☐
Local Community Group	☐	☐	☐	☐
General Practitioner	☐	☐	☐	☐

Clergy (Priest/ Minister)	☐	☐	☐	☐
Other Individual and/or Organisation (Specify)	☐	☐	☐	☐

_____

Have there been any <u>unsuccessful</u> attempts by intruders to enter your home without permission? This applies to any house you have lived in this area (i.e.).

Yes ☐   No ☐   **IF NO, GO TO NEXT**
IF YES, PLEASE SPECIFY
....
....

How many times in last 12 months?
0 ☐   1 ☐   2 ☐   3 ☐
4 ☐   5+ ☐

On the last occasion, were the police informed?
Yes ☐   No ☐   Don't know/NA ☐

Did you seek help from:	Yes	No
Friends / Relatives	☐	☐
Local Community Group	☐	☐
General Practitioner	☐	☐
Clergy (Priest/ Minister)	☐	☐
Other Individual and/or Organisation (Specify)	☐	☐

_____

None of the above	☐	☐

If yes, how helpful did you find them to be?
     [*Use categories: Very helpful, Helpful, Not helpful at all, DK*]

Friends / Relatives	☐	☐	☐	☐
Local Community Group	☐	☐	☐	☐

General Practitioner	☐	☐	☐	☐
Clergy (Priest/ Minister)	☐	☐	☐	☐
Other Individual and/or Organisation (Specify)	☐	☐	☐	☐

_____

A few questions now about anything that may have been stolen from or vandalised *outside* the house.

Apart from milk, bicycles or motor vehicles, have you ever had anything <u>stolen</u> from outside your property - e.g. from the doorstep, garden or garage - while you have been living in this area (i.e.)?

Yes ☐   No ☐   **IF NO, GO TO NEXT**

How many times in last 12 months?

0 ☐   1 ☐   2 ☐   3 ☐
4 ☐   5+ ☐

Did you seek help from:	Yes	No
Friends / Relatives	☐	☐
Local Community Group	☐	☐
General Practitioner	☐	☐
Clergy (Priest/ Minister)	☐	☐
Other Individual and/or Organisation (Specify)	☐	☐
_____		
None of the above	☐	☐

If yes, how helpful did you find them to be?

  [*Use categories: Very helpful, Helpful, Not helpful at all, DK*]

Friends / Relatives	☐	☐	☐	☐
Local Community Group	☐	☐	☐	☐
General Practitioner	☐	☐	☐	☐
Clergy (Priest/ Minister)	☐	☐	☐	☐

Other Individual and/or ☐ ☐ ☐ ☐
Organisation (Specify)
_____

Has anyone <u>deliberately damaged or vandalised</u> the outside of your property (including gardens, sheds and fences but not bicycles or vehicles) while you have lived in this area?
Yes ☐   No ☐   Don't know/NA ☐
IF NO, GO TO NEXT
IF YES, PLEASE SPECIFY
....
....

How many times in last 12 months?
0 ☐   1 ☐   2 ☐   3 ☐
4 ☐   5+ ☐

On the last occasion, were the police informed?
Yes ☐   No ☐   Don't know/NA ☐

Did you seek help from: Yes   No
Friends / Relatives   ☐   ☐
Local Community   ☐   ☐
Group
General Practitioner   ☐   ☐
Clergy (Priest/   ☐   ☐
Minister)
Other Individual and/or   ☐   ☐
Organisation (Specify)
_____
None of the above   ☐   ☐

If yes, how helpful did you find them to be?
   [*Use categories: Very helpful, Helpful, Not helpful at all, DK*]
Friends / Relatives   ☐   ☐   ☐   ☐
Local Community   ☐   ☐   ☐   ☐
Group
General Practitioner   ☐   ☐   ☐   ☐

Clergy (Priest/ Minister)	☐	☐	☐	☐
Other Individual and/or Organisation (Specify) _____	☐	☐	☐	☐

ALL RESPONDENTS
[Only Asked if <u>didn't</u> inform police of any incident]
[Show list]
The following incidents happened to you and you <u>did not</u> inform the police. Choose the most serious of these incidents that occurred...
In your decision <u>not</u> to inform the police, were any of the following reasons a consideration?

	Yes	No
Private, personal or family matter	☐	☐
Dealt with it myself (ourselves)	☐	☐
Reported to other authorities (eg company security staff etc.)	☐	☐
Reported to Republican / Loyalist groups	☐	☐
Dislike / fear of police	☐	☐
Fear of reprisal by offenders/ make worse	☐	☐
Police could do nothing	☐	☐
Police would not have bothered/not interested	☐	☐
Inconvenient/too much trouble	☐	☐
No loss damage	☐	☐
Attempt at offence was unsuccessful	☐	☐
Did not want to attract attention by having police here	☐	☐
Too trivial/not worth reporting	☐	☐
other (specify)_____		

What was your main reason for <u>not</u> informing the police (given list if reasons above, pick one)

[List]

Of the incidents which happened to you and you <u>did</u> inform the police - thinking of the <u>most serious</u> incident that occurred... [ask to rank the most serious from list of incidents that occurred]
Can you tell me about the way in which the police responded?
ie. did you have to wait at all before the police <u>attended</u> the matter, or did they respond immediately?
Had to wait? ☐ Responded immediately? ☐ Police never responded? ☐
Not applicable/victim did not want to be involved further? ☐ (skip following if this response)

Did the length of time you had to wait seem reasonable to you or not? A reasonable time? ☐ Not a reasonable time? ☐

How much <u>interest</u> did the police show in what you/he/she had to say?
As much as you thought they should? ☐
less than you thought they should? ☐

How much <u>effort</u> would you say the police put into dealing with the matter, was it?
As much as you thought they should? ☐
less than you thought they should? ☐

How well did they keep you (the victim) <u>informed</u> of the progress of their investigations. Was it?
Very well? ☐ fairly well? ☐ Not very well? ☐
Not at all well? ☐

How polite were they in dealing with you (the victim). Were they
Very polite? ☐ Fairly polite? ☐ Fairly impolite? ☐
Very impolite? ☐

Overall, were you (the victim) satisfied or dissatisfied with the way the police handled the matter?
Very satisfied? ☐ Fairly satisfied? ☐ A bit dissatisfied? ☐
Dissatisfied? ☐ Too early to say? ☐

Did this contact with the police make you feel more or less favourable to the police in general or did it make no difference to your view of them?

More favourable? ☐   Less favourable? ☐   No difference? ☐

CRIME PREVENTION
I would like to ask you some questions about crime prevention.
Has your home been security upgraded with....
Does your house have them? [then, if 'yes']
Did you install them?

	Yes	No	Install
Stronger doors	☐	☐	☐
Improved locks on doors or windows	☐	☐	☐
Security chain on door	☐	☐	☐
Burglar alarm	☐	☐	☐
Security lighting on outside of house or block	☐	☐	☐
Erection of fences or entrance gates around ground floor entrance	☐	☐	☐
Resident caretaker in multis	☐	☐	☐
Spyhole in door	☐	☐	☐
Entry phone	☐	☐	☐
Buy Dog	☐	☐	☐

If you did one of the above because you were worried about crime, was that worry based on?

	Yes	No
Personal experience of crime	☐	☐
Police advice	☐	☐
Friends or neighbours	☐	☐
Community group or voluntary organisation advice	☐	☐
TV programme, eg, Crimewatch	☐	☐
Advertising	☐	☐
Other please specify	☐	☐

Do you normally <u>inform</u> neighbours or relatives if you are leaving the house empty for a while,   e.g.,   holidays?

	Yes	No	Don't know	NA (eg doesn't leave home)
Neighbours?	☐	☐	☐	☐
Relatives?	☐	☐	☐	☐
Friends	☐	☐	☐	☐
No one	☐	☐	☐	☐
DK /NA	☐	☐	☐	☐

Would you normally <u>inform</u> the police if you were leaving the house empty?
Yes ☐   No ☐   Don't know/NA ☐

Would you normally ask any of the following to <u>come in to check</u> the house? (eg. when on holiday)

	Yes	No	Don't know/NA
Neighbours?	☐	☐	☐
Relatives?	☐	☐	☐
Friends?	☐	☐	☐
Police	☐	☐	☐
No one	☐	☐	☐

[Question asked only if more than one resident in house]
When you go out do you ensure there is someone in the house?
Always ☐ Sometimes ☐ Never ☐ NA ☐

Are the contents of your house insured against theft?
Yes ☐   No ☐   Don't know/NA ☐

IF YES, Have you claimed for any theft in last 12 months?
Yes ☐   No ☐   Don't know/NA ☐

IF NO, Why not insured? (Tick any that apply)
Property not worth insuring ☐
Insurance too expensive ☐
Insurance cover refused ☐
Haven't got around to it ☐
Too complicated ☐
Other (please specify) ....

Have you ever received threatening or abusive phone calls?
If so, did you inform anyone (please
specify)...

PARENTAL CONCERNS
We want to move on to issues concerning your children and their safety in general terms. Are you the parent or guardian of children under the age of 18 living in this household?
Yes ☐   No ☐   **IF NO, GO TO NEXT SECTION**
[Information to be taken from Household Grid]

Are you the parent/guardian of any children living in this house, aged?
Number
Under 5 years ☐
5-11 years ☐
12-15 years ☐
16-17 years ☐

In comparison with most other areas in Northern Ireland, how good is it around here to bring up children?
Better ☐   About same ☐   Worse ☐   Don't know ☐

[If more than one child in any age category, eldest chosen]
Do any of your children go out to local play areas, open spaces and streets to play by themselves, (that is, without an adult)?
Yes ☐   No ☐   **IF NO, GO TO NEXT**

If yes, where do they play? (please specify)
Under 5 years ....
5-11 years   ....
12-15 years   ....

How safe do you think your children are when they go out to play by themselves?
Under 5 years
Very safe? ☐ Fairly safe? ☐ Not very safe? ☐ Not at all safe ☐
5 - 11 years
Very safe? ☐ Fairly safe? ☐ Not very safe? ☐ Not at all safe ☐

12 - 15 years
Very safe? ☐ Fairly safe? ☐ Not very safe? ☐ Not at all safe ☐

Do you allow your children out to school or the shop **alone**?
	During the day?		At night?
Under 5	Yes ☐	No ☐	N/A ☐
5-11	Yes ☐	No ☐	N/A ☐
12-15	Yes ☐	No ☐	N/A ☐

Do you worry about them when they are out alone (without an adult)?
Under 5
A lot ☐ Quite a lot ☐ A little ☐ Not at all ☐ not allowed out ☐
5-11
A lot ☐ Quite a lot ☐ A little ☐ Not at all ☐ not allowed out ☐
12-15
A lot ☐ Quite a lot ☐ A little ☐ Not at all ☐ not allowed out ☐
16-17
A lot ☐ Quite a lot ☐ A little ☐ Not at all ☐ not allowed out ☐

Did you worry more or less about your children during the cease-fires?
more ☐   less ☐   no difference ☐   don't know ☐

If you have children aged 5-15
Including school based activities, what out of school hours activity are your children involved? (Do not include summer holiday schemes etc.)
To be looked at in above age group categories
(a)   sports clubs /leisure centres
(b)   school activities
(c)   community organised activities and clubs
(d)   church organised activities and clubs
(e)   privately organised and funded activities
(f)   visiting friends' houses
(g)   mixing with friends in public places <u>in this area</u> (including the street, around the shops, etc.)
(h)   mixing with friends in public places in <u>other</u> areas other (specify) _____

How important is safety (as opposed to educational value, fun, cost, child's preference etc.) in your decision about your child's activities? (Using age categories)
Most important? ☐ Quite important but not central? ☐
Fairly important? ☐ Neutral? ☐ Not considered? ☐
[Show Card]

Do you worry about the possibility of the following specific things when they are out alone (without a responsible adult)?

A lot=1 Quite a lot=2 A little=3 Not at all=4 N/A=5

    1   2   3   4   5

Playing in dangerous places
5-11 ☐ ☐ ☐ ☐ ☐
12-16 ☐ ☐ ☐ ☐ ☐

Being run over by motor vehicles
☐ ☐ ☐ ☐ ☐
☐ ☐ ☐ ☐ ☐

Being bullied by other children
☐ ☐ ☐ ☐ ☐
☐ ☐ ☐ ☐ ☐

Being a nuisance to other people
☐ ☐ ☐ ☐ ☐
☐ ☐ ☐ ☐ ☐

Playing truant from school
☐ ☐ ☐ ☐ ☐
☐ ☐ ☐ ☐ ☐

Getting involved with drugs or gluesniffing
5-11 ☐ ☐ ☐ ☐ ☐
12-16 ☐ ☐ ☐ ☐ ☐

Having things stolen from them
☐ ☐ ☐ ☐ ☐
☐ ☐ ☐ ☐ ☐

Being sexually molested
☐ ☐ ☐ ☐ ☐
☐ ☐ ☐ ☐ ☐

Being bullied or hit by adults
☐ ☐ ☐ ☐ ☐
☐ ☐ ☐ ☐ ☐

Being attacked by dogs
☐ ☐ ☐ ☐ ☐
☐ ☐ ☐ ☐ ☐

Getting into fights with other youngsters
☐ ☐ ☐ ☐ ☐
☐ ☐ ☐ ☐ ☐

Vandalising property
☐ ☐ ☐ ☐ ☐
☐ ☐ ☐ ☐ ☐

Drinking alcohol
☐ ☐ ☐ ☐ ☐
☐ ☐ ☐ ☐ ☐

Getting into trouble with the police
☐ ☐ ☐ ☐ ☐
☐ ☐ ☐ ☐ ☐

Hassled by the police
☐ ☐ ☐ ☐ ☐
☐ ☐ ☐ ☐ ☐

Joining gangs
☐ ☐ ☐ ☐ ☐
☐ ☐ ☐ ☐ ☐

Getting involved with paramilitaries
☐ ☐ ☐ ☐ ☐
☐ ☐ ☐ ☐ ☐

Being hassled by paramilitaries
☐ ☐ ☐ ☐ ☐
☐ ☐ ☐ ☐ ☐

When your children finish school for the day, are they supervised by an adult? (eg. at home, at a relative /child minder, friends house)
yes ☐   no ☐

ALL RESPONDENTS
5.   COMMUNITY GROUPS AND CRIME PREVENTION
Could I now ask you some questions about Your Community and Prevention of Crime around here.
How satisfied are you, generally speaking, with the service provided around here by:

Very satisfied (1)   Satisfied (2)   Unsatisfied (3)
Very unsatisfied (4)   Don't know/NA (5)

	1	2	3	4	5
Housing Executive	☐	☐	☐	☐	☐
Social Services	☐	☐	☐	☐	☐
Street Cleansing Department	☐	☐	☐	☐	☐
Community Centres	☐	☐	☐	☐	☐
Residents Association	☐	☐	☐	☐	☐
Parks Department	☐	☐	☐	☐	☐
Police	☐	☐	☐	☐	☐

The police perform a number of different duties. I'll go through a list of these. Could you please tell me how important each should be for the police locally and how good the police are at each of these duties.

AFTER COMPLETION OF LIST   NOW, how good are the police at each of these duties?

HOW IMPORTANT: 1   2   3   4
HOW GOOD: 1   2   3

Involvement in community projects (eg. school visits etc)	☐	☐	☐	☐
Walking the beat	☐	☐	☐	☐
Patrolling in cars	☐	☐	☐	☐
Providing crime prevention advice	☐	☐	☐	☐
Responding to emergency calls	☐	☐	☐	☐
Visiting schools and youth clubs	☐	☐	☐	☐
Checking security of shops and public facilities	☐	☐	☐	☐
Controlling dogs	☐	☐	☐	☐
Investigating terrorist or sectarian crime	☐	☐	☐	☐

Dealing with drug problems ☐ ☐ ☐ ☐
☐ ☐ ☐
☐ ☐ ☐

Do you think that the police understanding of people's problems around here is:-
Good ☐ Average ☐ Poor ☐ Don't know ☐

Do you know any police officers around here, either to speak to or by sight?
To speak to ☐   By sight ☐
No, neither ☐

In the last 12 months, have you contacted a police officer?
   Yes ☐   No ☐

IF NO, GO TO NEXT
   HOW?   By phone ☐   In person ☐
   Other ☐

WHY (on last occasion)?
   Report a crime ☐
   Traffic problem ☐
   Noise/nuisance ☐
   Missing person ☐
   For advice/help ☐
   Other(specify)____

Were you satisfied with the way the police treated you? Yes ☐
   No ☐

How likely or unlikely would you be to report any of the following incidents to the police?

VERY LIKELY	FAIRLY LIKELY	FAIRLY UNLIKELY	VERY UNLIKELY	N/A D/K

Having your home broken into
☐   ☐   ☐   ☐   ☐
Deliberate damage to the outside of your house

☐ ☐ ☐ ☐ ☐
Someone stealing something you were carrying
☐ ☐ ☐ ☐ ☐
Someone assaulting or attacking you - with fists, kicks or weapons
☐ ☐ ☐ ☐ ☐
Someone threatening to hurt you or to damage your property or Possessions
☐ ☐ ☐ ☐ ☐
(VEHICLE OWNERS ONLY)
Theft from your vehicle
☐ ☐ ☐ ☐ ☐

POLICING

How polite are the police in your area?
very polite ☐
quite polite ☐
neither polite nor impolite ☐
quite impolite ☐
very impolite ☐
DK/NA ☐

How <u>fairly</u> do the police treat people <u>in your area</u> when dealing with problems.
(using scale)
Very fairly ☐ quite fairly ☐ neither fairly nor unfairly ☐
quite unfairly ☐   very unfairly ☐

Please tell me how you think the police treat Catholic and Protestant members of the public in Northern Ireland
Catholics treated much better ☐
Catholics treated a bit better ☐
Both treated equally ☐
Protestants treated a bit better ☐
Protestants treated much better ☐
Don't know /refusal ☐

If you had a complaint against the police (eg. for verbal abuse, or physical assault), who do you think you could report it to? [Don't prompt]

Specify_____

How likely would it be that you would report it to;
Very Likely, Likely, Neither likely nor unlikely, Unlikely, Very Unlikely

Police ☐ ☐ ☐ ☐ ☐
Police Authority ☐ ☐ ☐ ☐ ☐
Solicitor ☐ ☐ ☐ ☐ ☐
Independent commission for police complaints
☐ ☐ ☐ ☐ ☐
Local politician ☐ ☐ ☐ ☐ ☐
Clergy/Community group ☐ ☐ ☐ ☐ ☐
Republican / Loyalist group ☐ ☐ ☐ ☐ ☐

Did your opinion of the police improve, worsen or remain much the same during the period of the cease fires?
Opinion has improved ☐   Opinion remained much the same ☐
Opinion worsened ☐   NA/no opinion ☐

Are there any other organisations who might deal with Crime in your area? Please specify.
....
....

Who deals with the following problems in your area? (eg. Community groups, residents associations, Loyalist / Republican groups, etc)
(a) Nuisances
(specify)_____
(b) Property/crime
(specify)_____
(c) Violent crime
(specify)_____

What do you think are the most important things that could be done to reduce crime and improve safety around here?
(egs, Better lighting, improve the appearance of the area, more police patrols, improvements in locks on doors windows etc, Video cameras, better facilities for young people, better relations between neighbours, etc.)
AFTER DISCUSSION, identify the 3 most important (in order)

1..
....
2..
....
3..
....

Victim Support
Victim Support Schemes are groups of volunteers trained to give information, help and advice to the   victims of crime. Had you heard of Victim Support before now?
Yes ☐   No ☐

Have you had contact with Victim Support because of any crime against you?
Yes ☐   No ☐

IF YES
What sort of contact did you have with Victim support? Was it:
Visit to home ☐   Telephone call ☐
Letter telling you how to obtain help if you wanted it   ☐

How helpful was the contact with Victim Support? Was it:
Very helpful ☐   Fairly helpful ☐
Not very helpful   ☐   not at all helpful   ☐

BACKGROUND
[1.1 to 1.5 asked at outset of interview in grid]
Can I ask a few background details about yourself and your home?
Age: .... (please state actual age)
Sex: Male ☐   Female   ☐

Marital Status?
Single   ☐
Married   ☐
Cohabiting   ☐

Separated ☐
Divorced ☐
Widowed ☐

Who else lives in this house and their relationship to you? (using grid)
....

....

....

Employment Status? (Using categories)
Working Full-time ☐
Working Part-time ☐
On a Government Training Scheme ☐
Retired ☐
Student (Further Education) ☐
Caring for children\relatives ☐
Other (Please Specify) ☐
_____
Presently unemployed ☐

What is/was the title of your present/most recent job? (please specify)
....

What is your income **before** tax and national insurance contributions? Include **all** income from employment, pensions and benefits, etc.

£............................ (show card with week, month, year breakdown)

RELIGION
How would you describe your religious tradition? (tick one only)
Protestant ☐   Roman Catholic ☐
None ☐   Other (specify) _____   Refused ☐

If Protestant which denomination?
C of I ☐   Presbyterian ☐
Methodist ☐   Baptist ☐

Free Presbyterian ☐   Other ☐
Refused ☐   None ☐

Do you attend church ?   Yes ☐   No ☐

If yes, how often ?
daily ☐   more than once a week ☐   weekly ☐
monthly ☐   less than once a month ☐
only on special occasions ☐ (eg. weddings, funerals)

How important is your religion in your life?
very ☐   quite important ☐   a bit important ☐
not at all ☐

OTHER ORGANISATIONS
Apart from the Church, do you belong to any other organisations that are important in your life
(eg. social clubs, voluntary organisations etc?)
Yes ☐   No ☐
(Please specify)
....
....

What is the most important?   (please specify)
....

How often would you be involved with this organisation?
Daily ☐   Weekly ☐   Monthly ☐
Other ☐ (please specify)..................................

Going out
Thinking about an average weekday how many hours do you spend outside your home during the day?
none   under 1   1 but under 3   3 but under 5
5 but under 7   7 or more

In the last seven days have you spent any evenings outside your home for any reason?

Yes ☐   No ☐

Which evenings were you out? (tick as appropriate)
Monday   ☐   Tuesday ☐   Wednesday ☐
Thursday   ☐   Friday   ☐   Saturday ☐
Sunday   ☐
 (If No)
You have not been out in the evening in the last seven days. How often do you usually go out after dark?
At least once a week   ☐
At least once a fortnight   ☐
At least once a month   ☐
Less often than once a month ☐
Never   ☐
(if 1.14= <1per month OR never)

You mentioned you never / rarely go out after dark.
Why do you never or rarely go out after dark? (tick most important)
Too old   ☐
Too sick/ill/disabled   ☐
Family responsibilities   ☐
Fear of crime to person ☐   Fear of burglary   ☐
Fear dark/night   ☐
Fear of going out on your own   ☐
No money   ☐
too expensive   ☐   Nowhere to go /nothing to do ☐
Busy working/content to stay in ☐   Don't want to go out ☐ No transport   ☐   other   ☐
(if 1.14b yes)

The last time you went out in the evening, what was the one main thing you did when you went out?
Paid work   ☐
Visit friends/relatives   ☐
Went to pub   ☐
Went to Cafe/restaurant   ☐
Went to party/dance/disco   ☐
Went to place of worship   ☐

Evening class ☐
Took part in Sport ☐
Went to club/committee ☐
Went to cinema/theatre ☐
Went to bingo ☐
Shopping ☐
Other ☐

Type of Dwelling? (Interviewer Observation)
Flat ☐
Terrace House ☐
Detached ☐
Semi-detached ☐

Is the home you live in?
Owned outright ☐
Owned with a mortgage ☐
Rented from a private landlord ☐
Rented from the Housing Executive ☐
Rented from a Housing Association ☐
Part owned, part rented ☐
Sheltered Accommodation ☐
Don't know ☐

And finally:
In view of the events of recent weeks, has your concern for your own safety, that of your family and property, changed to what you felt before the docklands bombing in London?
Are you now:
A lot more concerned ☐
a little more concerned ☐
About the same ☐
Less concerned ☐
A lot less concerned ☐
DK ☐

[Show card]

In view of those events, would you say the problems identified earlier <u>when taken as a whole</u> should...

Improve a lot	☐
Improve	☐
Remain the same	☐
Get worse	☐
Get a lot worse	☐
DK	☐

CLOSE INTERVIEW AND THANK RESPONDENT

Bibliography

Anderson B. (1991) *Imagined Communities*. London: Verso.
Anderson S., Grove Smith C., Kinsey R. & J. Wood (1990) *The Edinburgh Crime Survey*. Edinburgh: University of Edinburgh.
Armstrong N. & McManus A. (1994) 'Children's fitness and physical activity among 11-16 year old British Children', *British Medical Journal*, 301, 203-205.
Barry A., Osborne T. & Rose N. (1993) *Economy and Society: Special Issue on Liberalism and Governmentality*. London: Routledge.
Barry A., Osborne T. and Rose N. (*eds.*) (1996) *Foucault and Political Reason: Liberalism, Neo-Liberalism and Rationalites of Government*. Chicago: University of Chicago Press.
Becker G. (1968) 'Crime and Punishment: An Economic Approach'. *Journal of Political Economy*, Vol. 76, p 128-147.
Beckett K. & Sasoon T. (1999) *The Politics of Injustice: Crime and Punishment in America*. London: Sage.
Belfast City Council (1999) 'Play Policy', visited 8th December 1999, at http://www.belfastcity.gov.uk/playpolicy.htm
Bell C. (1996) 'Alternative Justice in Ireland' in N. Dawson, D. Greer and P. Ingram (*eds.*) *One Hundred and Fifty Years of Irish Law*. Belfast: SLS Publications.
Bennett T. & Wright R. (1984) *Burglars on Burglary*. Aldershot: Gower.
Bottomley A. & Pease K. (1986) *Crime and Punishment: Interpreting the Data*. Milton Keynes: Open University Press.
Bottoms A., Mawby R. & Walker M. (1987) 'A Localised Crime Survey in Contrasting Areas of a City'. *British Journal of Criminology*, Vol. 27, p 125-154.
Bowyer Bell J. (1993) *The Irish Troubles: A Generation of Violence*. Dublin: Gill & MacMillan.
Box S., Hale C. & Andres G. (1988) 'Explaining Fear of Crime' in *British Journal of Criminology*, Vol. 28, No. 3, 340-356.

Boyle M. & Haire T. (1996) *Fear of Crime and Likelihood of Victimisation in Northern Ireland.* Research Findings. November 1996. Belfast: Northern Ireland Office, Statistics & Research Branch.

Breen R. (1995) 'Attitudes towards the Security Forces'. In Breen R., Devine P. & Robinson G. (*eds.*) *Social Attitudes in Northern Ireland: The Fourth Report.* Belfast: Blackstaff Press.

Brewer J. (1993) 'Public Images of the Police in Northern Ireland' in *Policing & Society,* Vol. 4, p 163-176.

Brewer J., Lockhart W. & Rogers P. (1997) *Crime in Ireland 1945-1995: Here be Dragons.* Oxford: Clarendon Press.

Brownlee I. (1998) 'New Labour – New Penology? Punitive Rhetoric and the Limits of Managerialism in Criminal Justice Policy', *Journal of Law and Society,* Vol. 25, 1, p 313-335.

Bruce S. (1992) *The Red Hand: Protestant Paramilitaries in Northern Ireland.* Oxford: Oxford University Press.

Bryett K. (1997) 'Does Drumcree '96 Tell us About the RUC?' *Critical Criminology,* Vol. 8, 1, p 49-62.

Bucke T. (1997) *Ethnicity and Contacts with the Police: Latest Findings from the British Crime Survey.* Research Findings No. 59. London: HMSO.

Burchell G., Gordon C. & Miller P. (1991) *The Foucault Effect: Studies in Governmentality.* Harverster Wheatsheaf: Hemel Hempstead.

Butcher H. (1993) 'Introduction: Some Examples and Definitions'. p 3-22 In Butcher H., Glen A., Henderson P. & Smith J. (*eds.*) *Community & Public Policy.* London: Pluto Press.

Cairns E. (1987) *Caught in Crossfire: Children and the Northern Ireland Conflict.* Appletree Press: Belfast.

Cale L. and Almond L. (1992) 'Physical activity levels of young children: a review of the evidence'. *Health Education Journal,* Vol. 51, 2, p 94-99.

Caul B. (1983) 'Juvenile Offending in Northern Ireland - A Statistical Overview'. In Caul B., Pinkerton J. & Powell F. (*eds.*) *The Juvenile Justice System in Northern Ireland.* Jordanstown: Ulster Polytechnic.

Census Office (1994) *The Northern Ireland Census 1991: A Guide to NI Census Statistics.* Belfast: Census Office for Northern Ireland.

Chambers G. & Tombs J. (1983) *The British Crime Survey: Scotland.* Edinburgh: HMSO.

Churches Report (1976) *Violence in Ireland: A Report of the Churches*. Belfast: Christian Journals.

Cloward R. & Ohlin L. (1960) *Delinquency & Opportunity: A Theory of Delinquent Gangs*. New York: Free Press.

Cohen A. (1985) *The Symbolic Construction of Community*. London: Tavistock.

Cohen A. (1987) *Whalsay, Symbol, Segment and Boundary in a Shetland Island Community*. Manchester: Manchester University Press.

Conway P. (1997) 'A Response to Paramilitary Policing in Northern Ireland'. *Critical Criminology*, Vol. 8, 1, p 109-122.

Coogan T. (1995) *The Troubles: Ireland's Ordeal 1966-1995 and the Search for Peace*. Hutchinson: London.

Crane J. (1982), 'Growing up Through the Troubles'. *The Listener*, 7th January 1982.

Crawford A. (1995) 'Appeals to Community and Crime Prevention'. *Crime, Law and Social Change*, Vol. 22, p 97-126.

Crawford A (1999) *The Local Governance of Crime: Appeals to Community Partnerships*. Oxford: Oxford University Press.

Crawford A., Jones T., Woodhouse T. & Young J. (1990) *The Second Islington Crime Survey*. Middlesex: Centre for Criminology.

Crow G. & Allan G. (1994) *Community Life: An Introduction to Social Relations*. Hemel Hempstead: Harvester Wheatsheaf.

Currie D., DeKerskey W. & MacLean B. (1990) 'Reconstituting Social Order and Social Control: Police Accountability in Canada'. *Journal of Human Justice*, Vol. 2, 1, p 29-54.

Currie E. (1998) *Crime and Punishment in America*. New York: H. Holt.

Dalley G. (1988) *Ideologies of Caring: Rethinking Community and Collectivism*. London: Macmillan.

Davidson A. (ed.) (1997) *Foucault and his Interlocutors*. Chicago: Chicago University Press.

De Keseredy W., MacLean B. & Schwartz M. (1997) 'Thinking Critically About Left Realism'. In MacLean B. & Milovanovic D., *Thinking Critically About Crime*. Vancouver: Collective Press.

Department of Transport (1995) *National Travel Survey 1992-4*. London: HMSO.

Ditton J., Short E., Philips S. & Khan F. (1994) *Safety in Castlemilk: 1994 Compared to 1990*. Glasgow: Scottish Centre for Criminology.

Dobash R. & Dobash R. (1979) *Violence Against Wives*. London: Tavistock.

Dobash R. & Dobash R. (1992) *Women, Violence and Social Change*. London: Routledge.

Ennis P. (1967) *Criminal Victimization in the United States: A Report of the National Survey*. U.S. Presidents Commission on Law Enforcement and the Administration of Justice Field Survey 11. Washington: GPO.

Foucault M. (1982) 'The Subject and Power'. In Dreyfus H. & Rabinow P. (*eds.*) *Michel Foucault: Beyond Structuralism and Hermeneutics*. Harverster Wheatsheaf: Hemel Hempstead.

Foucault M. (1991) 'Governmentality'. In Burchell G., Gordon C. and Miller, P. (*eds.*) *The Foucault Effect: Studies in Governmentality*. Harvester Wheatsheaf: Hemel Hempstead, p 87-104.

Foucault M. (1997) 'The Ethics of the Concern of the Self as a Practice of Freedom'. In Rainbow P. (*ed.*) *Michel Foucault: Ethics*. Penguin Books: Harmondsworth.

Gallagher A. (1995) 'Policing in Northern Ireland: Attitudinal Evidence'. In O'Day A. (*ed.*) *Terrorism's Laboratory*. Aldershot: Dartmouth.

Garland D. (1996) 'The Limits of the Sovereign State'. *The British Journal of Criminology*, Vol.36, p 445-471.

Garland D. (1997) 'Governmentality and the Problems of Crime: Foucault, Criminology, and Sociology'. *Theoretical Criminology*, Vol. 1, p 173-214.

Garofalo J. (1979) 'Victimisation and the Fear of Crime'. *Journal of Research in Crime and Delinquency*, Vol. 16, p 80-97.

Geary R. & Morison J. (1993) 'Studying Crime & Conflict: The Northern Ireland Example'. In *Northern Ireland Legal Quarterly*, Vol. 44, 1, p 65-70.

Geary R. & Morison J. (1993) 'The Perceptions of Crime' in P. Stringer & Robinson J. (*eds.*) *Northern Ireland Social Attitudes Survey 1992*. Belfast: Blackstaff Press.

Geary R. & Morison J. (1996) 'An Illustration of the Literary Approach to the Study of Law: The "Mysteries" Novels of the Nineteenth Century and the "Troubles Thriller"'. In Dawson N., Ingram, P. & Greer D. (*eds.*) *150 Years of Irish Law: Queen's 150th Anniversary Essays*. Dublin: Roundhall, p 105-124.

Geddis P. (*ed.*) (1997) *Focus on Northern Ireland: A Statistical Profile.* The Stationary Office: London.

Gordon C. (1991) 'Governmental Rationality'. In Burchell G., Gordon C. & Miller P. (*eds.*) *The Foucault Effect: Studies in Governmentality,* Harvester Wheatsheaf: Hemel Hempstead, p 1-52.

Hacking I. (1990) *The Taming of Chance.* Cambridge: Cambridge University Press.

Hacking I. (1991) 'How should we do the history of statistics?' in *The Foucault Effect: Studies in Governmentality,* G. Burchell, C. Gordon and P. Miller (*eds.*) Hemel Hempstead: Harvester Wheatsheaf.

Hale C. (1996) 'Fear of Crime: A Review of the Literature'. *International Review of Victimology,* Vol. 4, p 211-233.

Hamilton A., Moore L. & Trimble T. (1995) *Policing in a Divided Society.* Centre for the Study of Conflict: University of Ulster.

Hanmer J. & Saunders S. (1984) *Well Founded Fear.* London: Hutchinson.

Hartnagel T (1979) 'The Perception and Fear of Crime: Implications for Neighbourhood Cohesion, Social Activity, and Community Affect'. Social Forces, Vol. 58, p 176-193.

Heskin K. (1981) 'Societal Disintegration in Northern Ireland: Fact or Fiction?' *The Economic and Social Review,* Vol. 12, p 97-113.

Hillman M., Adams J. and Whitelegg N. (1990) *One False Move: A Study of Children's Independent Mobility.* London: Policy Studies Institute.

Hillyard P. (1985) 'Popular Justice in Northern Ireland: Communities & Change'. In S. Spitzer (*ed.*) *Research in Law, Deviance & Social Control,* Vol. 7, Connecticut: JAI Press.

Hobbs D. (1988) *Doing the Business: Entrepreneurship, the Working Class and Detectives in the East End of London.* Oxford: Oxford University Press.

Hood R. & Sparks R. (1970) *Key Issues in Criminology.* London: Weidenfeld & Nicholson.

Hope T. & Shaw M. (1988) 'Community Approaches to Reducing Crime' in Hope T. & M. Shaw (*eds.*) *Communities and Crime Reduction.* London: HMSO.

Hough M. & Mayhew P. (1983) *The British Crime Survey.* Home Office Research Study No. 76. London: HMSO.

Hough M. (1995) *Anxiety about Crime: Findings from the 1994 British Crime Survey.* HORS, Research Findings No. 25. HMSO: London.

Hunt A. & Wickham G. (1994) *Foucault and Law: Towards a Sociology of Law and Governance*. London: Pluto Press.

Jones H., Short D. & Berry W. (1994) *Dundee N.E. Safer Cities Project 1994. Household Survey Report*. Edinburgh: Scottish Office Central Research Unit.

Jones T., MacLean B. & Young J. (1986) *The Islington Crime Survey: Crime, Victimisation and Policing in Inner City London*. London: Middlesex Polytechnic.

Kinsey R. (1984) *Merseyside Crime Survey: First Report*. Liverpool: Merseyside Metropolitan Council.

Kippax F. (1993) *Other People's Blood*. Fontana: London.

Koffman L. (1996) *Crime Surveys and Victims of Crime*. University of Wales Press: Cardiff.

Labour Force Survey (1994) *Religion Report*. Northern Ireland Statistics and Research Agency: Belfast.

Light R. (1993) *Car Theft: The Offender's Perspective*. Home Office Research Study No. 130. London: HMSO.

MacLean B. (1991) 'In Partial Defense of Socialist Realism: Some Theoretical and Methodological Concerns of the Local Crime Survey'. *Crime Law & Social Change*, Vol. 15, 3, p 213-254.

Maguire M. (1997) 'Crime Statistics, Patterns & Trends: Changing Perceptions & Their Implications'. In Maguire M., Morgan R. & R. Reiner (eds) *The Oxford Handbook of Criminology* (2nd ed.) Oxford: Clarendon Press, p 135-189.

Mathews R. & Young J. (eds) (1986) *Confronting Crime*. London: Sage.

Mayhew P. and van Dijk J. (1997) *Criminal Victimisation in Eleven Industrialised Countries. Key Findings from the 1996 International Crime Victims Survey*. The Hague: WODC.

Mayhew P., Aye Maung N. & Mirrlees-Black C. (1993) *The 1992 British Crime Survey*. Home Office Research Study 132. HMSO: London.

McCauley M. & Cunningham G. (1983) 'Intermediate Treatment and Residential Treatment for Juvenile Offenders in Northern Ireland.' In Caul B., Pinkerton J. & F. Powell (eds) *The Juvenile Justice System in Northern Ireland*. Jordanstown: Ulster Polytechnic.

McCullough D., Schmidt T. & Lockhart B. (1990) *Car Theft in Northern Ireland: Recent Studies on a Persistent Problem*. Extern: Belfast.

McEvoy K., McElrath K. & Hoggins K. (1998) 'Does Ulster Still Say No? Drugs, Politics and Propaganda in Northern Ireland'. *Journal of Drug Issues*, Vol. 28, 1, p 127-154.

McEvoy K. & Mika H. (1998) 'Restorative Justice, Punishment & Praxis: Non-violent Alternatives to Paramilitary Punishments in Northern Ireland'. ASC: Washington (paper presented at the American Society of Criminology Conference, November 1998).

McGarry J. & O'Leary B. (1999) *Policing Northern Ireland: Proposals for a New Start.* Belfast: Blackstaff Press.

McLaughlin E. (1993) 'Women & the Family in Northern Ireland: A Review'. In *Women's Studies International Forum.* Vol. 16, 6, p 553-568.

McVeigh R. (1994) *Its Part of Life Here: The Security Forces and Harassment in Northern Ireland.* Belfast: Committee on the Administration of Justice.

Miles R. (1994) *The Children we Deserve: Love and Hate in the Making of Families.* London: Harper Collins.

Miller P. & Rose N. (1990) 'Governing Economic Life'. *Economy and Society*, Vol. 19, p 1-19.

Mirrlees-Black C. & Allen J. (1998) *Concern about Crime: Findings from the 1998 British Crime Survey.* HORS Research Findings, No. 83. HMSO: London.

Mirrlees-Black C., Budd, T., Partridge S. & Mayhew P. (1998) *The 1998 British Crime Survey.* HMSO: London.

Mirrlees-Black C., Mayhew P. & Percy A. (1996) *The 1996 British Crime Survey, England & Wales.* Home Office Statistical Bulletin Issue 19/96. Home Office Research & Statistics: London.

Morison J. & Geary R. (1989) 'Crime Conflict & Counting: Another Commentary on Northern Ireland Crime Statistics' in *Howard Journal*, Vol. 28, 1, p 9-26.

Morison J. (1995) 'Putting Crime in Northern Ireland in an International Perspective.' In L. Kennedy (*ed.*) *Crime & Punishment in West Belfast.* Belfast: the Summer School.

Morison J. (2000) 'The Government-Voluntary Sector Compacts: Governance, Governmentality, and Civil Society'. *Journal of Law and Society*, Vol. 27, p 98-132.

Morison J. & Livingstone S. (1995) *Reshaping Public Power: Northern Ireland and the British Constitutional Crisis.* London: Sweet & Maxwell.

Morrissey M. & Pease K. (1982) 'The Black Criminal Justice System in West Belfast'. *The Howard Journal,* Vol. 21, p 159-166.

Mulcahy A. (1999) 'Visions of Normality: Peace and the Reconstruction of Policing in Northern Ireland'. *Social and Legal Studies,* Vol. 8, p 277-295.

Munck R. (1988) 'The Lads and the Hoods: Alternative Justice in an Irish Context'. In Tomlinson M., Varley T. & McCullagh C. (*eds.*) *Whose Law & Order?* Belfast: Sociological Association of Ireland.

Murray C. (1984) *Losing Ground: American Social Policy 1950-1980.* New York: Basic Books.

New Law Journal (1983) 'Editorial: Crime in Northern Ireland.' In *New Law Journal,* Vol. 132, p 401-402.

Northern Ireland Office (1976) 'Northern Ireland Office Circular re. Juvenile Delinquency.' Cited in B. Caul (1983) *Juvenile Offending in Northern Ireland - A Statistical Overview.* Jordanstown: Ulster Polytechnic.

Northern Ireland Office (1993) *Crime and the Community.* Belfast: HMSO.

Northern Ireland Office (1997) *Crime & Criminal Justice in Northern Ireland.* NIO Home Page Internet. Website http://www.nio.gov.uk

O'Farrell C. (*ed.*) (1997) *Foucault: The Legacy.* Brisbane: Queensland University of Technology.

O'Mahony D., McEvoy K., Geary R., Morison J. & Brogden M. (1997) *The Northern Ireland Communities Crime Survey.* School of Law, Institute of Criminology and Criminal Justice, Queen's University of Belfast.

O'Mahony D. & Quinn K. (1999) 'Fear of Crime and Locale: The Impact of Community Related Factors upon Fear of Crime'. *International Review of Victimology,* Vol. 6, p 231-251.

O'Mahony D. & Quinn K. (2000) *The Community Dimension on Attitudes Towards the Police: A Report for the Police Authority for Northern Ireland.* Belfast: Police Authority for Northern Ireland.

O'Malley P. (1991) 'Legal Networks and Domestic Security'. *Studies in Law, Politics and Society,* Vol.11, p 171-190.

O'Malley P. (1992) 'Risk, Power and Crime Prevention', *Economy and Society*, Vol.21, p 252-275.

O'Malley P. (1996 *a*) 'Risk and Responsibility'. In Barry A., Osborne T. and Rose N., *Foucault and Political Reason*, Vol Press: London, p 189-207.

O'Malley P. (1996 *b*) 'Indigenous Governance'. *Economy and Society*, Vol. 25, p 310-326.

O'Malley P., Weir L. & Shearing L. (1997) 'Governmentality, Criticism, Politics', *Economy and Society*, Vol. 26, p 501-517.

Painter K. (1991) *Wife Rape, Marriage and the Law: Survey Report*. Manchester: University of Manchester Faculty of Economics and Social Science.

Park R. (1937) 'Human Ecology' in *American Journal of Sociology*, Vol. 42, 1, p 1-15.

Parker H. (1974) *View from the Boys*. Newton Abbot: David Charles.

Patten C. (1999) *Report of the Independent Commission on Policing for Northern Ireland, A New Beginning: Policing in Northern Ireland*, HMSO: London.

Pavlich G. (1996) *Justice Fragmented: Mediating Community Disputes under Post-modern Conditions*. London: Routledge.

Petit L. (1996) *The Psalm Killer*. Macmillan: London.

Police Authority Northern Ireland (PANI) (1996) *A Partnership for Change: A Report on Further Consultation by the Police Authority for Northern Ireland*. PANI: Belfast.

Police Authority Northern Ireland (PANI) (1998) *Reflecting All Shades of Opinion: Part Two The Findings*. Belfast: Police Authority for Northern Ireland.

Powell F. (1982) 'Justice and the Young Offender in Northern Ireland'. *British Journal of Social Work*, Vol. 12, p 565-586.

Robson B., Bradford M. & Deas I. (1994) *Relative Deprivation in Northern Ireland*. Occasional Paper No. 28. Policy, Planning & Research Unit: Belfast.

Rose N. & Miller P. (1992) 'Political Power Beyond the State: Problematics of Government'. *British Journal of Sociology*, Vol. 43, p 173-205.

RUC (1980) *Annual Report of the Chief Constable*. Belfast: RUC.

RUC (1997) *Report of the Chief Constable 1996/1997*. Belfast: RUC.

RUC (1999) *Report of the Chief Constable 1998/1999*. Belfast: RUC.

Ryan M. (1999) 'Penal Policy Making Towards the Millennium: Elites and Populists: New Labour and the New Criminology'. *International Journal of the Sociology of Law*, Vol. 27, 1, p 1-22.

Scottish Office (1998) *Main Findings from the 1996 Scottish Crime Survey*, Edinburgh: Central Research Unit.

Scottish Office (1998) *Main Findings from the 1996 Scottish Crime Survey*, The Scottish Office: Edinburgh.

Shaw C. & McKay R. (1942) *Juvenile Delinquency in Urban Areas*. Chicago: Chicago University Press.

Shense J. (1999) 'Creating Space for Change: Can the Voluntary Sector Help End Northern Ireland's Troubles?' *Harvard Human Rights Journal*, Vol. 11, p 149-161.

Skogan W. (1990) *The Police and Public in England and Wales: A British Crime Survey Report*. HORS. No. 134. London: HMSO.

Smandych R. (ed.) (1999) *Governable Places: Readings on Governmentality and Crime Control*. Aldershot: Gower.

Sparks R., Genn H. & Dodd D. (1977) *Surveying Victims*. Chichester: Wiley.

Sparks R. (1992) *Television and the Drama of Crime*. Buckingham: Open University Press.

Stanko E. (1988) 'Hidden Violence Against Women'. In Maguire M. & J. Pointing (eds.) *Victims of Crime: A New Deal?* Milton Keynes: Open University Press.

Stenson K. (1993) 'Community Policing as a Governmental Technology'. *Economy and Society*, Vol. 22, p 373-389.

Van Dijk J., Mayhew P. & Killias M. (1990) *Experiences of Crime Across the World*. Deventer: Kluwer.

Van Dijk J. & Mayhew P. (1992) *Criminal Victimisation in the Internationalized World: Key Findings of the 1989 and 1992 International Crime Surveys*. The Hague: Netherlands Directorate for Crime Prevention, Ministry of Justice.

Van Dijk J. (1994) 'Understanding Crime Rates'. *The British Journals of Criminology*, Vol.34, p 105-121.

Walklate S. (1996) 'Community & Crime Prevention' in McLaughlin E. & J. Muncie (eds.) *Controlling Crime*. London: Open University Press.

Weir L. (1996) 'Recent Advances in the Government of Pregnancy'. *Economy and Society*, Vol. 25, p 373-392.

Wheway R. and Millward, A. (1997) *Child's Play: Facilitating Play on Housing Estates.* Coventry: Charted Institute of Housing.

Whyte J. (1990) *Interpreting Northern Ireland.* Oxford: Oxford University Press.

Willmott P. (1987) 'Introduction'. In P. Willmott (*ed.*) *Policing and the Community.* London: Policy Studies Institute.

Wilson J. & Herrnstein (1985) *Crime and Human Nature.* New York: Simon & Schuster.

Winston T. (1997) 'Alternatives to Punishment Beatings and Shootings in a Loyalist Community in Belfast'. *Critical Criminology,* Vol. 8, 1, p 122-128.

Young J. (1988) 'Risk of Crime and Fear of Crime: The Politics of Victimisation Studies'. In M. Maguire & J. Pointing (*eds.*) *Victims of Crime: A New Deal.* Milton Keynes: Open University Press.